LOCAL GOVERNMENT
IN ACTION

Local Government in Action
A Simulation
WORKBOOK

Bill Kennedy & Gary N. Wilson

UNIVERSITY OF TORONTO PRESS

Copyright © University of Toronto Press 2014
Higher Education Division

www.utorontopress.com

Previously published by Broadview Press 2008 © Bill Kennedy and Gary N. Wilson

Library and Archives Canada Cataloguing in Publication

Kennedy, Bill
        Local government in action : a simulation : workbook / Bill Kennedy & Gary N. Wilson.

ISBN 978-1-55111-912-0

        1. Municipal government—Canada—Simulation games. I. Wilson, Gary N. (Gary Norman), 1967–
II. Title.

JS1710.K45 2008   320.8'50971   C2008-901981-4

We welcome comments and suggestions regarding any aspect of our publications—please feel free to contact us at news@utphighereducation.com or visit our Internet site at www.utppublishing.com.

North America
5201 Dufferin Street
North York, Ontario, Canada, M3H 5T8

2250 Military Road
Tonawanda, New York, USA, 14150

ORDERS PHONE: 1-800-565-9523
ORDERS FAX: 1-800-221-9985
ORDERS E-MAIL: utpbooks@utpress.utoronto.ca

UK, Ireland, and continental Europe
NBN International
Estover Road, Plymouth, PL6 7PY, UK
ORDERS PHONE: 44 (0) 1752 202301
ORDERS FAX: 44 (0) 1752 202333
ORDERS E-MAIL: enquiries@nbninternational.com

The University of Toronto Press acknowledges the financial support for its publishing activities of the Government of Canada through the Canada Book Fund.

CONTENTS

ACKNOWLEDGEMENTS

This simulation arose from a belief that our Public Administration Certificate Program students at the University of Northern British Columbia could benefit from a simulation that would help them learn about the kinds of issues that affect northern and resource communities in Canada. During the course of preparing a simulation for our own use, we came to realize that the simulation might be of use to others who teach courses related to local governance. This material is the result of discussions with colleagues in academia and in local government about the types of issues and characters that should be included in such a simulation.

In particular, we would like to acknowledge the assistance and support of our colleagues at the University of Northern British Columbia: thanks go to John Young, Boris DeWiel, and Tracy Summerville. Jason Morris provided a great deal of assistance in the earlier development of the simulation. We are indebted to the students of POLS 260—Local Government Finance (Spring 2007) for piloting an earlier version of this simulation and helping us to work out some of the kinks. Three reviewers from Broadview Press provided very helpful suggestions, some of which we have been able to incorporate. We are also grateful for the support and encouragement of Greg Yantz and the editorial assistance of Karen Taylor at Broadview.

The support given to the Public Administration Certificate Program by the Len Traboulay Education Fund was also important to the development of the simulation.

Finally, we would like to thank our wives and families for their support and encouragement and for their tolerance of our work on the manuscript on too many spring and summer weekends and evenings.

Bill Kennedy
Gary Wilson

TWO
Introduction

This is a simulation about a fictional, medium-sized municipality. It is intended to provide a teaching tool that deals explicitly with the governance of small and medium-sized communities in Canada, and that focuses on the major issues faced by resource-based communities and by communities on the peripheries of metropolitan areas.

Simulations can be an excellent way of demonstrating what real decision making is like, and they can give students some experience of dealing with competing interests, conflicting points of view, and the occasional clash between "common sense solutions" and the actions that are permissible under law.

The goals and objectives of this simulation are

1. To simulate reality in a way that allows students to grasp the complexity of arriving at solutions to local issues (illustrating points such as the complexity of issues, competing demands of residents, conflicting goals of residents, local vs. provincial and national interests);

2. To show students the processes involved in council meetings and, if there are sufficient participants, the processes involved when advisory bodies provide recommendations to council;

3. To make students aware of the role of municipal staff and the nature of the relationship between elected officials, appointed officials, and the public; and

4. To illustrate the practical applications of the theories and concepts learned in class.

As in the case of any well-constructed simulation, this exercise will offer students the opportunity to "practise" the skills required to make effective presentations, to participate in decision-making meetings, to lobby, to observe, and to report. It will also allow them to make their instructor more aware of their character and capabilities (which can be useful for student evaluation or when references are sought).

This simulation is not intended to produce "winners" and "losers," although, as in real life, there will be some who will feel that they have "won" or "lost." By and large, there are no "right" answers to the issues that are posed, except in the sense that the "right answer" is the answer that is acceptable to the residents of our fictional municipality. In other words, the instructor and the authors do not have a "crib sheet" with an "approved" solution for each issue. It is up to those who are on the Summerville's city council, and those who advise and lobby them, to develop a solution that is acceptable to the majority of the community members.

In this simulation, a number of you will participate as members of the Summerville City Council, as members of the city's administration, and as community developers and activists. Others will participate as business managers, residents, or members of community groups. Your instructor will assign the role that you are to play. Together, you will address a variety of issues that are typical of those faced by the citizens of small and medium-sized communities.

While Summerville is a fictional community, and the characters and issues raised in the simulation are fictional, the characteristics of the community and the nature of the issues have been based on situations found in real municipalities. In this sense, the issues are "real" and, it is hoped, will give you a "real" experience of the challenges facing communities and the local governments that administer them.

THREE
Workbook Organization

Local Government in Action—A Simulation will require that you participate in the civic life of the fictional community of Summerville. Your participation may be very active, as a member of the council or of the city's administration or as a developer or civic activist, or it may be less active. Just as in a normal community, in Summerville, you will find various levels and types of civic involvement.

This book is a tool that will enable you to participate effectively in the simulation. It is not intended to be a "script" for your role, to tell you what you should do or say. It does give you information on the various characters that live and work in Summerville. You will be expected to play the role of at least one of the characters. This information (together with information that the instructor may provide to you) is to be used by you to develop the character that you have been assigned to play. The book also gives important information about Summerville, about the laws under which Summerville operates, about the issues facing Summerville, and, most important, about the way in which the simulation will be conducted.

The book begins with a description of how the simulation is organized (Section 4). This section tells you how the council is structured, how the business of the community is conducted, how time is calculated for the simulation, and how the simulation starts. It also tells you about the local newspaper, the *Summerville Sentinel,* and the role of the instructor as the newspaper reporter. The following sections (5 through 8) provide more detailed information on how council meetings are organized and conducted, and on the organization of the council meetings that will take place during the simulation.

Section 9 provides background information on the community of Summerville, including a description of its geography, history, and demographics. This is followed by a description of the various issues that might be addressed by the Summerville City Council (Section 10), an outline of the cast of characters (Section 11), and information about the rules and regulations governing elections in Summerville (Section 12). The book concludes with appendices that include the procedure bylaw that governs the conduct of the council meetings, extracts of provincial legislation that apply to Summerville, and forms that are used in the simulation.

The simulation is organized around a series of council meetings. As each meeting approaches, you will want to check the agenda and determine if the issues that appear on the agenda in any way affect the character or role that has been assigned to you. For example, you may be playing the role of a resident of an area that is affected by a zoning matter that will be discussed by the council. You may wish to appear before the council to present your views, or you may wish to contact the proponent of the project to obtain further information or negotiate some change to the project. The description of your character will give you hints about the positions that your character might take. Keep in mind that you are playing a role in the simulation and that the views you may be called upon to express will not necessarily be your own.

If you are required to make a presentation to council (either to gain permission to do something, or to have something done, or to try to persuade council not to do something), it will be necessary for you to prepare your presentation in advance. You will want to study the information about the community, the issue at hand, and the views of other characters that may be affected by the issue. You will also want to make a presentation that puts your position forward in a favourable light and that, at the same time, anticipates the arguments that others may make against your position. If you are playing the role of a member of the city's administration, you will want to read the description of the character, of his or her duties, and of the issues in which the character is involved, and familiarize yourself with the legislation and procedural rules that govern the official's work.

FOUR
Simulation Organization

Local Government in Action—A Simulation is centred on the business of the Summerville City Council. This does not imply that all of the major decisions about life in Summerville or any community are made at the council table. Many decisions affecting cities such as Summerville are made outside the community (by entrepreneurs in corporate boardrooms, by provincial and federal politicians and bureaucrats, and by investors) and within the community (by individuals, by other local agencies such as school boards, by local organizations such as churches and service clubs, by local businesses, and by local managers of national and multinational companies). In short, the city council is but one of many bodies that make decisions affecting community life. However, city council is one of the most important, as the city has the legal power to undertake many activities that, for better or worse, shape the community. These activities include regulating land use and development, regulating the behaviour of the residents of the community, providing municipal services, and protecting people and property. The simulation has been designed to bring forward the decisions and views of the wide variety of groups that affect life in a community without trying to simulate all of their decision-making processes.

You will find descriptions of the major components of this simulation in the following pages. These pages are intended to give you an overview of the simulation. More detailed information on council meetings, the issues, the characters, and the community will be found in subsequent sections.

4.1   Council Meetings

As indicated above, the Summerville City Council meetings are the focus of this simulation. The city council meets every other week. (See Section 4.6 for a discussion of "simulation time.") At these meetings, councillors deal with a variety of issues that may appear on the council agenda for any number of reasons. A municipal council serves at least three roles:

1. As the legislative body for a community, enacting laws to regulate community affairs, subject to the constraints of the provincial legislation that established the municipality

2. As the executive or governing body for the bureaucracy that is employed to provide municipal services to the community

3. As an assembly of elected officials that can legitimately make political statements about issues that affect the community

As you will see in Section 5, council meetings are conducted in a formal way, according to procedural rules that determine the order of business. The meeting is chaired by the mayor (or, in Summerville's case, the acting mayor). Only members of council participate in the discussion and debate. Members of the administration may, from time to time, answer questions posed by members of the council, or they may bring to council's attention information that may be of assistance to council. Members of the public may be invited to address council, either as a delegation or during the course of a public hearing. However, when it comes to reaching a decision on the issue before the council, only members of council are entitled to debate the issue and to vote on any relevant motions.

When acting as a legislative body (that is, when considering the enactment of a by-law), the council may be required by provincial legislation to follow certain procedures. Those procedures may involve giving notice to the community or property owners regarding the council's intent to enact a by-law or providing opportunities for public input prior to enacting the by-law. The legislative requirements for these processes must be followed with precision. Failure to follow the correct procedures can result in the courts striking down the by-law (in effect, saying that the by-law is not valid). Appendix 2 contains extracts from the legislation governing councils' procedures, and it can be referred to for guidance.

There are occasions when the council is required to hear and consider evidence relating to an issue or issues on its agenda. Examples include hearing the views of the public on proposed by-laws (such as in the case of public hearings on rezoning by-laws) or when council is considering revoking or refusing a privilege or a licence. In such instances, the council is said to be acting in a "quasi-judicial" role, and there are strict requirements with respect to fairness and avoidance of bias or discrimination. Council members are expected to keep an open mind until they have heard all points of view. They are also required to avoid entering into private discussions or receiving input (written or verbal) that is not public. Failure to follow appropriate procedures may open the council to legal proceedings that could invalidate its decisions.

Unlike the boards of corporations, a municipal council makes decisions in public. There are strict rules governing what types of issues can be dealt with in private. These are described in the legislative extracts in Appendix 2. In general, all council meetings must be public (which means that the public and the media have a right to be present) except for those that deal with personnel issues, legal matters (such as notice of writs filed against the municipality, legal advice from staff or the city solicitor, and advice about the legality of planned policies or projects, as well as advice on cases currently before the courts), or issues such as land sales where the premature release of information about the municipality's position could harm its economic interests.

Each council meeting is conducted according to an agenda. The agenda lists the issues to be considered by the council and the order in which they will be considered. If the council is not prepared to reach a decision (for example, if members require more information or if they wish to obtain the views of a community group), the council can postpone a decision by "tabling" the issue to a future meeting. Alternatively, council can refer the matter to the administration, requesting that the administration study the issue and bring back a report.

The relationship between members of the municipal council and the municipality's administration is a complex one. Council members are elected to set municipal policy and to generally direct the business of the municipality. However, they are seldom experts in the various facets of municipal government and must rely on "expert" advice from a variety of sources, but primarily from members of their administration. It used to be said that the role of council was to set policy and the role of the administration was to implement policy. However, the boundaries between policy creation and implementation are often difficult to determine. The relationship between council and administration is usually dynamic and involves dialogue, interplay, and collaboration. Most reports to council from administration can be regarded as part of that process. Generally, they contain factual information, a description of possible courses of action, an evaluation of the probable outcomes of the courses of action, and, last, a recommendation. Ultimately, however, council has the final decision-making authority.

The agenda for each council meeting will be determined by the person assigned to play the role of the municipal clerk, and it will include issues that are either designated in this book or decided by the instructor.

4.2   Roles

While by-laws, legislation, and agendas constitute an important part of council meetings, it is the individuals involved that truly shape the meetings. *Local Government in Action; a Simulation* provides for a variety of roles, each with unique characteristics. Each participant will be assigned a role to play in the simulation. Depending on class size and the nature of the role, some individuals may play more than one role. The instructor, based on information provided by you about your interests, will assign the roles. A listing of the roles can be found in Table 4.1. The nature and characteristics of each role are explained in more detail in Section 11 (Roles). The roles used in your simulation will depend on the issues that your instructor chooses to include in the simulation and on the number of people participating in the simulation.

One of the advantages of a simulation is that it provides an opportunity to experiment and to take on roles that you might not normally seek.

Therefore, you should not hesitate to play roles such as a member of council or of the administration. However, the roles of property developer, business owner, homeowner, and others are also essential to the success of the simulation, and you should not overlook them as an opportunity to gain "hands on" experience in seeking to influence public policy.

You may not (in fact, you probably will not) be assigned to a role that perfectly fits your interests, points of view, or personality. It is expected that you will, to the extent possible, act in the way suggested in the description of your role. This will require that you think about how different types of people would view the issues before the council, and how they would respond in order to bring others around to their points of view. Professional acting ability is not required, but you may have to express views that are not necessarily your own in order to play the role appropriately.

The description of the roles and the outline of the issues contain hints that you can use to develop the role that you have been assigned. For example, the description of an issue may indicate that your character is opposed to a particular issue. The description of the role outlines aspects of your character's political and personal beliefs and social and economic circumstances. By melding these two sources of information, you will be able to determine a course of action that you should take in playing your role.

A "cast of characters" is suggested for each issue, but it should not be taken as limiting participation only to those mentioned. Summerville is a democracy, and all residents who have an interest in an issue are entitled to express their opinions and influence the development of public policy, provided that they do so within the applicable procedures and laws. Therefore, you should feel free to examine the issues coming before council and identify any that you feel would be of interest to your character. This interest could be expressed by appearing at public hearings, forming alliances (for example, making an alliance to support another character's position on a particular issue in return for that person's support of your position on another issue), or lobbying members of council or the administration.

4.3   Issues

During the course of the simulation, the Summerville City Council will be presented with a number of issues to consider. These issues are the heart of the simulation. They involve consideration of the interests of the community at large, as well as the interests of the municipal corporation, and the balancing of competing viewpoints, interests, and perspectives. Information on the issues can be found in Section 10. Not all the issues will be considered during the course of the simulation. Your instructor will choose which issues to include.

TABLE 4.1 List of Roles*

ESSENTIAL (NON-SHAREABLE ROLES)	HIGHLY INVOLVED ROLES	ROLES THAT CAN BE SHARED	ADDITIONAL ROLES
1 Councillor #1	8 Beautician	18 Auto Wrecker	31 Councillor #5
2 Councillor #2	9 Building Contractor	19 "Big Box" Developer	32 Councillor #6
3 Councillor #3	10 Building Inspector	20 Chair, Chamber of Commerce	33 Elementary School Teacher
4 Councillor #4	11 Chair, Recreation Commission	21 Door Maker	34 City Planner
5 City Administrator	12 Hardware Store Owner	22 Librarian	35 Casino Developer
6 City Clerk	13 Public Health Inspector	23 Massage Therapist	
7 City Treasurer	14 President, Fire Fighters' Union	24 Pub and Motel Owner	
	15 Real Estate Developer	25 Ridgeview Drive Resident	
	16 Riverside Anglican Church Minister	26 Riverside Acres Owner	
	17 Solicitor	27 Royal Heights Resident	
		28 Speedy Taxi Driver	
		29 Sports Parent	
		30 Wild Flower Lady	

*Not including the role of Newspaper Reporter, which is to be played by the instructor.

4.4   Newspaper

As is the case in many communities, the business of the municipality features prominently in the local newspaper. The Newspaper Reporter (your instructor) is responsible for choosing the news to report. The news may be only what happens at council, or it may include some investigative reporting to identify conflicts and alliances within the community that are not readily evident at council meetings. If the simulation is held over a couple of days, the news will be presented to the community immediately before the opening of each council meeting. If the simulation is held over several weeks, news bulletins can be emailed to you or posted on a website.

4.5   Starting the Simulation

Summerville has suffered the loss of a very popular mayor (returned to office by acclamation at the last municipal elections). Consequently, the first business before the Summerville City Council is to elect an acting mayor from among the members of council. The by-election for the office of mayor is to be held in fourteen weeks, with nomination day being ten weeks away.

The council also must proceed diligently with finalization of the city's annual budget in order to meet the statutory deadlines for adopting a budget and enacting the by-laws that are required to impose the annual property tax levy.

Therefore, the instructor will call the first council meeting to order with the expectation that the council will begin to address the issues before it as expeditiously as possible. Fortunately, the previous mayor had worked closely with the city's administration, and the agendas and issues to be dealt with at the next two council meetings are set (see Section 6 and 7 of the workbook).

You will need to do some preparation for the first council meeting. The nature of that preparation will depend on the role that you have been assigned, but, at the very least, it should include the following:

» Read Section 1 through 6 of this workbook

» Read Section 9 and 11 (read the parts that deal with your assigned role particularly carefully)

» Read the background material on the issues to be dealt with at the first two council meetings in Section 10 (read the issues in which your character is involved with particular attention)

» Read Section 13.1 and 13.2 (the appendices)

You may also wish to read additional material in textbooks on local government, watch a televised council meeting or two, or even go to a council meeting in person.

As the simulation progresses, you will have to review the election processes (described in detail in Section 12). You will also need to continue reading the material on the issues that are to be dealt with at each council meeting. In preparing to participate in the discussion of these issues, you may want to consult texts, journals, newspapers or magazines, or use the Internet to obtain information on how other municipalities have dealt with similar issues.

As you begin the simulation, it is important to remember that you are playing the role assigned to you and that your colleagues are also playing roles. Remember that positions taken by others (and yourself) may not (and probably do not) reflect their personal views or perspectives.

4.6   Simulation Time

The Summerville City Council meets every two weeks. Therefore, for the purpose of the simulation, we assume that there is a two-week interval between council meetings (even though, in real time, the interval may range from a matter of hours to a week, depending on class schedules). When you see reference to "two weeks" in this workbook, you should interpret this as being the interval between one council meeting and the next meeting and not fourteen real days.

FIVE

Conducting a Council Meeting

Municipal council meetings are the forum for municipal politics. As such, they should be conducted in a dignified manner appropriate to decision making that affects the economic interests of the community and the property and individual rights of the community's inhabitants. Council meetings are, therefore, conducted with a fair amount of formality, but with perhaps less formality than would be found in parliament or other legislative assemblies. The following sections will present some basic information about council meeting rules of order and agendas and also some practical suggestions about how a member of council can bring an idea to council for consideration, how a citizen can bring an issue before council, and, finally, how a citizen can make his or her views known at a public hearing.

5.1   Rules of Order

To an outsider, the rules of order of a council meeting often seem to impede discussion and slow the deliberations of the body. The rules, however, have a number of important purposes, in addition to making sure that appropriate decorum is preserved. They help individuals to work with each other in a harmonious fashion, protect the ability of a member of the council to state positions or ideas that might not be favoured by the majority, and support due process in the adoption of legislation.

We have all probably, at one time or another, left meetings believing that our time was wasted, that nothing productive was achieved, or feeling that we insulted, put down, or marginalized. The rules of order for council meetings are intended to avoid dysfunctional behaviours that can sometimes occur during meetings. They are set out in some detail in a bylaw that governs council procedures. The council procedure by-law for Summerville can be found in Appendix 1.

The procedures impose a certain form of conduct on the participants. First, the chair of the meeting (the mayor or acting mayor) retains control of the meeting. The chair determines who speaks, and when. Members cannot just begin speaking when there is a lull in the conversation. They must "catch the eye" of the mayor (by raising their hand at an appropriate time or through some other visual clue, sort of in the manner of a bidder at an auction), and they must wait until they are invited to speak. If there is a debate on an issue, the mayor will keep a "speakers list" of those members of council who have indicated that they wish to speak. When one speaker has concluded, the mayor will invite another member to speak by saying something along the lines of "Councillor X is next" or "Councillor Y has the floor." The mayor can interpret the rules of order, or points of order, that are raised by members of council, but his or her decisions are subject to appeal to the council as a whole. In general, the expectation is that council members will gather their thoughts before speaking on an issue and that they will speak only once (although there are usually provisions or opportunities for rebuttal or summarization). The mayor also determines what is to be discussed. In general, discussions arise only when there is a motion on the floor (and when that motion is debatable). If there is an issue on the agenda and no member of the council makes a motion to deal with the issue (such as a motion to receive a letter, to approve a request, or to adopt a resolution), the mayor would simply move on to the next item on the agenda. Once a motion is on the floor (which means that members of council can discuss the motion), the mayor's job is to ensure that members are, in fact, talking about the motion that is before council and not about some other issue. In other words, councillors must stick to the point.

Second, council members do not talk to each other. They address the mayor. This convention has two purposes: it helps to maintain order, and it serves to avoid personal arguments. Since all members must address their comments to the mayor (in a manner similar to that followed by elected representatives in the provincial or federal legislatures), the mayor has an opportunity to make sure that councillors are waiting their turn to speak and that they are only speaking on the issue before council. If they are speaking out of turn (that is, when someone else has the floor) or if they are not speaking to the issue before council, the mayor can rule them "out of order," which means that they must immediately cease speaking. The convention that members of council speak to the chair and not to each other helps to depersonalize the dialogue and avoid the strong emotions that can arise when two individuals begin to argue with each other. Strong emotions are still expressed at council meetings, but this convention helps to keep such feelings under control.

Third, only council members participate in the debate. Members of the staff may be invited to provide information to council, or even to give their opinions on an issue, but that is at the invitation or indulgence of council. Staff members do not, by their presence, have a right to participate in a debate with an aim to influence the outcome. Nevertheless, it should be stressed that a wise council is one that ensures that the expertise of staff is available to councillors through verbal or written presentations to council. Similarly, the public does not have the right to participate in council debates. Members of the public may be invited to make presentations to council, and they have the right to speak when the council is holding a hearing (such as at a public hearing on a rezoning by-law). Council meetings are, with certain exceptions, open to the public, which means that members of the public and the media can be in attendance and observe the proceedings. In order to participate in the debates of council, however, a person must first be elected to council.

Fourth, certain standards of language and decorum are expected. Generally, "unparliamentary" language is prohibited. The use of profanity, obscenities, and vulgar language is not allowed. Similarly, members of council are not allowed to make derogatory comments about other members that impugn their motives or question their honesty.

Finally, there is an agreed order of business. Rather than hopping from topic to topic in random order, the procedure by-law specifies the order in which certain types of issues are to be addressed. The agenda for the meeting provides detailed information about the issues to be discussed.

5.2   Order of Business and Agendas

Each council meeting is conducted according to a particular order of business that is set out in the council procedure by-law. Within a predefined framework, provision is made for consideration of minutes of prior meetings, correspondence directed to council, reports, hearings, by-laws, and other items. The listing of items to be dealt with at each meeting is referred to as the "agenda." Procedure by-laws generally require that the agenda is made available to council and the public in advance of the meeting and that items cannot be added to the agenda without the consent of council.

The agenda is usually prepared by the city clerk in consultation with the administrator and the mayor. The clerk needs to make sure that

» The minutes of the previous meeting are included in the agenda, so they can be adopted (with any necessary corrections);

» Any issues that have been tabled (deferred) by council are included in the agenda, if the council has specified a date or if reports, correspondence, or other information required for consideration are available for council;

» Items that have to be dealt with according to a legislative timetable are included in appropriate agendas (for example, the adoption of the budget and taxation by-laws); and

» Council policies with respect to hearing delegations and conducting hearings are observed.

For some meetings, it will be clear that there are too many items on the agenda and that the council is unlikely to be able to complete the agenda. In such cases, the clerk, in consultation with the mayor and administrator, may defer items to a later council meeting (depending on the council's policy). If, during a council meeting, councillors find that they cannot deal with all the agenda items in the time available, they can select items to be tabled for consideration at the next or some other, subsequent council meeting.

5.3   How to Get a Motion Considered by Council

People who get elected to council generally seek office because they want to achieve something, which means getting the council to agree either to do something or to stop something from being done. Council members have no power as individuals. Council's will is expressed by resolutions or motions adopted by a majority of the members. Consequently, to achieve something, a member of council must convince other councillors to vote in favour of his or her proposal. In order to do this, the councillor must present a motion for council's consideration.

There are several ways in which this can be done. If an item is on the agenda, the member of council can move a motion. For example, if there is a letter from a resident asking that a pothole be fixed, a council member can move a motion to have it fixed. The member might say, "I move that the director of public works arrange to have the pothole fixed." If another member of council agrees, or at least thinks the matter worthy of discussion, that member would say, "I second the motion." The motion is then said to be "on the floor" for discussion by council. If another member of council doubts that the pothole needs to be fixed, that member can move that the matter be tabled, pending receipt of a report from the director of public works about the size of the pothole. If a seconder is obtained, the tabling motion is put to a vote (a motion to table something is not debatable). If a majority of council votes in favour of tabling the motion, the debate ceases and the matter is not considered again until the report from the director of public works is available. At that time, council will vote on a motion to "lift the motion from the table." A motion to "lift from the table" requires a mover and a seconder. This type of motion is usually dealt with without debate. The original motion (to have the pothole fixed) is now before council for debate.

If a member of council feels that a motion should be somewhat different than the one that is "on the floor," he or she can move an amendment. For example, if a member felt that the pothole issue is urgent, that member could move an amendment to add the words "by noon tomorrow" so that the motion would read "that the director of public works arrange to have the pothole fixed by noon tomorrow." If another member of council is prepared to second the amendment, it would be considered by council before councillors vote on the original motion. In other words, council would consider whether the amendment should be adopted. If the amendment is adopted, council would eventually vote on the "motion as amended." If no one agrees that the pothole should be fixed by noon tomorrow and there is no seconder for the amendment, the mayor would declare that the "amendment failed for lack of a seconder." In that case, debate would continue on the original motion, and, eventually, the council will either adopt or defeat the motion by a vote.

If an issue is not on the agenda for a council meeting, a council member must arrange for the matter to be placed on the agenda. Generally, councils make some provision (time permitting) for members to raise new, non-contentious issues. This is often done at the end of a meeting, with the mayor giving each member a chance to raise something or to ask a question. Often, council members use these opportunities for the "good news" stories that they want to publicize. For example, one member of council might mention that she was at a sporting event where a local team won a championship, and another might say that he attended someone's 60th wedding anniversary or a charity event where a lot of money was raised. Council members also use these opportunities to ask questions of staff, sometimes with the purpose of trying to get more publicity for an issue or concern and sometimes because they want to raise the political profile of an issue and force debate or action. An example of the first purpose might include asking how well the city is doing in implementing a program to increase energy conservation. In such instances, the member of council probably knows the answer but wants to have the answer stated publicly, in the hope that the media will pick it up and turn it into a "good news" story for the city. An example of the second purpose might include asking the same question, but with the knowledge that the city has not done anything. A public admission that nothing has been done may give the council member an opportunity to launch a public debate about the need for energy conservation in city operations.

If the matter that the councillor wishes to introduce is a contentious issue, or one that the member of council wishes to address in some detail, the member can provide "notice of motion." Notice of motion is simply a device for a member to create a debate on a particular motion. For example, if a member wanted the council to consider requiring all dogs to be on leashes in parks, the member could give notice of a motion to do that, and the motion would be put on the agenda for the next council meeting. When the motion comes up for debate at that meeting, the member of council would then move the motion. If some other member of council seconds this motion, it would be debated and voted on by the council. The procedure by-law has specific provisions for notices of motion.

5.4   How to Bring an Issue to a Vote

In most instances, there is little disagreement or little discussion about motions. In many cases, a vote on a motion (and especially routine procedural motions) is held without any discussion. The mayor, seeing that there is no debate, would call for those in favour to show their hands, for those against to show theirs, and then announce the results. In other cases, the mayor may sense that discussion is complete or that it is becoming repetitive and non-productive. In such cases, it is the mayor's prerogative to "call the question" and to ask those in favour to raise their hands and then those opposed to raise theirs. Of course, if the mayor tries to shut off debate too early, he or she may be challenged. It is also the right of members of council to ask the mayor to "call the question," which means that they want the mayor to call a vote on the motion.

The art of chairing a meeting comes into play in establishing a speaking order and determining when to bring a discussion to an end. The mayor's role is to maintain order so that a civilized exchange of views can take place and the members of council have a reasonable opportunity to express their views on the issues before the council. The mayor has to take care not to block a member of council unreasonably from participating in the debates of council. At the same time, he or she must attempt to ensure that no one member of council unreasonably dominates the debate (or, in other words, hogs the microphone). The mayor can exercise a fair amount of discretion in this regard but must always remember that, under the rules of procedure, members of council have the right to challenge the mayor's rulings.

5.5   How to Bring an Issue to Council

Many citizens have the urge, from time to time, to complain to council about the way municipal services are provided or to ask council to adopt or refrain from adopting certain policies or objectives, but few actually do so. Often, they hold back because they are unsure of the procedures. There are several ways in which citizens can bring an issue to council.

One is to make personal contact with a member of council and attempt to persuade that individual to raise the issue in a council meeting. This approach is often used in smaller communities, where the residents are often friends, colleagues, neighbours, relatives, employers, or employees of members of council, or where they have regular contact with members of council through their churches, service clubs, teams, or other community activities. Making personal contact might involve a phone call, a discussion over a cup of coffee at the kitchen table, or a formal meeting with the member of council.

A second method is a letter to council. A letter, addressed to "His Worship the Mayor and Members of Council," can be used to convey a request, a suggestion, or simply a comment. In order to be sure that the letter actually gets on the council agenda, you should address the letter to the council as a group. A letter sent to the mayor as an individual, to an individual member of council, or to the city clerk may not necessarily be placed on the council agenda. Because of the volume of correspondence, most municipalities do not put correspondence on the council agenda unless it is clear that the correspondence is intended for council as a whole.

A third method of bringing an issue before council is for an individual to make arrangements to appear at a council meeting and make a verbal presentation. Many councils have established procedures to allow the public to appear at the beginning or end of council meetings to make such short presentations. As well, most councils have procedures whereby members of the public can make arrangements through the city clerk to appear as a delegation. Because of time constraints, the amount of time available for a presentation will be limited, and the council has the right to choose not to hear the presentation. Usually, councils will have established guidelines about receiving delegations and allowing personal presentations at council meetings. Persons wanting to appear before council should consult the city clerk.

A fourth method is to discuss the matter with a member of the city's administration. In certain cases, particularly where there are legal or highly technical matters involved, it may be more practical to work with the administration to have an issue brought forward to council. The procedures will vary depending on the circumstances, but they will probably involve a letter from the citizen to the administration, which would go forward to council accompanied by a report from the administration.

The methods available to individuals are also available to groups. Given time constraints, it is more likely that a council would agree to hear a presentation by a group of people rather than a series of presentations by individuals. One advantage of group presentations is that they can serve as a "signal" to council that there is a body of like-minded individuals that feel strongly about an issue. This indication of community interest can be helpful to council in evaluating public opinion and in gauging the political implications of taking decisions in response to the group's requests.

When considering whether to bring an issue before a municipal council, an individual or group must remember that, unless there are truly exceptional circumstances, the presentation will be made in public. This means that members of the public will be able to witness the presentation, either in person or by watching television coverage of the meeting. Further, the media may be present. Therefore, the individuals or groups making presentations will want to make sure that they do not divulge any confidential information, violate any other person's or group's right to privacy, or say anything that could be deemed slanderous. People need to remember that they will be held accountable for anything that they say in such a presentation and that they may be challenged if they make inaccurate or inappropriate representations.

5.6   How to Make Views Known at a Public Hearing

Public hearings are held to provide those who consider their interests to be affected by a matter with an opportunity to express their views on the subject of the hearing. In general, the council will interpret the concept of "interest" broadly. Therefore, participation in a hearing on a rezoning is not restricted only to those people who live close to the affected property or area. Others in the community may participate, but they must be able to show how the matter at hand affects their interests.

There are two ways in which an individual's views can be made known at a public hearing. One is by a written submission, which would be "read into" the hearing by the city clerk. The other way is by appearing in person to make a statement. All submissions (verbal or written) must be made in public. In the case of rezoning or community plan alterations, these open proceedings allow the proponent (the person who has asked for the rezoning) to know why people oppose the application and to rebut any points that they have made.

Public hearings on land use matters usually begin with city officials providing an overview of the proposed land use. The applicant for the change is then afforded an opportunity to present the case for approval of the application. Once these steps are completed, written submissions are read into the record, and the mayor calls on those who wish to make presentations to do so. If there are relatively few people interested in making presentations, the mayor determines the order in which they make their remarks to council. If there are a large number of people wishing to make presentations, it is common to make arrangements to have people register to indicate their desire to speak at the hearing. The mayor calls the people to make their representations in the order in which they had registered. If it is evident that a large number of people wish to make essentially the same point, the mayor may request that they appoint a single spokesperson to avoid a lot of time being taken up by identical, repetitious presentations. When there are no more people wishing to make representations, the mayor invites the applicant to make closing comments. This part of the process provides the applicant with an opportunity to either rebut arguments made by others or to provide additional information that would be helpful to his or her case.

Once everyone has been heard, a member of council moves a motion to close the public hearing. After closure of the public hearing, the council cannot receive any further information about the application (except for responses to certain technical questions that they may direct to staff), and the council begins to consider what to do about the application. At this point, council is said to be in the "debate stage." Aside from staff providing answers to technical questions, only members of council are eligible to speak during the debate.

As mentioned earlier, a public hearing is referred to as a "quasi-judicial" proceeding. This means that the way in which the hearing is conducted must meet certain standards for fairness, lack of bias, and openness. If it can be shown that the members of council were biased, that members of the public were not given reasonable access to present their views, or that the hearings were conducted in a manner that was not fair, either the applicant or an aggrieved citizen could apply to the courts to have the council's decision quashed.

SIX

The First Council Meeting

The simulation begins with the first meeting of the council. Although elections to fill the deceased mayor's position will take place in less than four months, the business of the city must continue. As a result, council has to appoint an acting mayor (who will act until a new mayor can be elected by the citizens of Summerville) and get on with the business of finalizing the budget for the current year. In addition, there are a number of development and economic issues to address. Consequently, the agenda for the first council meeting is full.

As is the case for all of the council meetings, you should study the agenda to see if your character is involved in any way with issues on the agenda (directly or indirectly). If you are directly involved, you will want to study up on the issue and determine what your obligations are. For example, in this first council meeting, the City Treasurer has to report to council on two matters: the deadline for adoption of the budget and the status of the budget deliberations to date. If you are indirectly involved, you may want to consider whether you should be lobbying members of council or staff, or perhaps other members of the community, in order to gain support for your issue or proposal.

You will see that all the staff reports fall under agenda item 8 (Report of the Chief Administrative Officer). It is common practice that all reports to council by city officials are submitted in the name of the chief administrative officer (after his or her agreement or approval) even if they have been prepared by other officials.

If it is not possible to deal with the agenda items by the end of the time allotted for the meeting, the unfinished items will have to be added to the agenda of the next council meeting. It is the responsibility of the City Clerk to keep track of any items that either are not addressed or are referred by council to subsequent council meetings; the Clerk must ensure that these items are included in future agendas in accordance with council's decisions.

As noted, the first issue Summerville's council has to face is the election of an acting mayor, who will serve until a new mayor can be elected. Members of the council will nominate a member of council to serve as acting mayor. Only members of council can be elected to the office of acting mayor. If more than one member of council is nominated to be acting mayor, a ballot will be held. The City Clerk will conduct the balloting. The Clerk will provide each member of council with a blank piece of paper. Members of council will write (or print) the name of the person that they want to vote for on the piece of paper. When all members of council have written down their choice, the City Clerk will collect the ballot papers, count the ballots, and announce the winner (the person with the most votes). If there is a tie and there are more than two candidates, the person with the lowest number of votes is dropped from the candidate list, and the process is repeated until someone gets more votes than anyone else. If there are two candidates and there is a tie vote, the candidates should toss a coin to determine the winner.

FIGURE 6.1 Agenda, Council Meeting #1

SUMMERVILLE CITY COUNCIL

Agenda
Council Chambers

1   **Call to Order**

2   **Approval of Agenda**

3   **Adoption of the Minutes of the Previous Council Meeting**

4   **Election of Acting Mayor**

5   **Introduction of Late Items**

6   **Public Hearings** (and third reading or adoption of by-laws where applicable)—Nil

7   **Delegations and Requests to Address Council**

    a)   A delegation requesting increased funding for the Summerville Secondary School Senior Girls Volleyball Team

8   **Report of the Chief Administrative Officer**
    a)   City Treasurer—Deadline for adopting the current year's budget
    b)   City Treasurer—Budget items for consideration by council

9   **Unfinished Business**—Nil

10 **Correspondence**
    a)   Request for a resolution endorsing "Gay Pride Day" and authorizing a "Gay Pride Rally" in Summerville City Centre Park

11 **Reports of Committee, COTW, and Commissions**—Nil

12 **Resolutions**
    a)   Resolution of congratulations to the Summerville Secondary School Senior Girls Volleyball Team

13 **By-laws**—Nil

14 **Question Period**

15 **New Business**

16 **Adjournment**

FIGURE 6.2 Minutes of the Previous Council Meeting

SUMMERVILLE CITY COUNCIL

City of Summerville
Minutes of the Meeting of Summerville
City Council Held On __ day of ____, 20__

Those present: Councillor #1, Councillor #2, Councillor #3, Councillor #4, City Administrator, City Clerk, City Treasurer

Absent: The Mayor

Call to Order: In the absence of the Mayor, Councillor #3 (the designated Acting Mayor pursuant to Section 7 of Council Procedure By-law) assumed the chair and called the meeting to Order at 7:05 pm.

Acceptance of the Agenda:
Moved by Councillor #1, seconded by Councillor #4, that the agenda for the meeting be accepted as presented.

Motion CARRIED

Minutes of the Last Meeting:
Moved by Councillor #2, seconded by Councillor #1, that the minutes of the last meeting be adopted as circulated.

Motion CARRIED

The Mayor:
The City Administrator advised Council that he had been informed by Mayor Russell's family that Mayor Russell was fatally injured in a car crash two nights ago and, in accordance with the Council Procedure By-law, it was necessary for Council to appoint a member of council as Acting Mayor until such time as an election can be held to elect someone to the office of mayor.

The City Clerk then presented a report setting out the recommendations for the election to fill the vacancy in the office of mayor, with the election proposed to be 14 weeks from the date of this council meeting.

Moved by Councillor #1, seconded by Councillor #4, that the recommendations of the City Clerk in respect of the election to fill the vacancy in the office of mayor be accepted in their entirety.

Motion CARRIED

Adjournment
Moved by Councillor #4 that, out of respect for the late Mayor Russell, the Council meeting adjourn.

Motion CARRIED

The meeting adjourned at 7:25 pm.

SEVEN

Council Meeting #2

Although the forthcoming by-election for mayor may be a major distraction for some members of council, the business of council must continue. The City Clerk should prepare an agenda for the second meeting. This agenda should look like the one in Figure 7.1. If there were any issues on the agenda for Council Meeting #1 that were not dealt with at that meeting, the Clerk will add them to the agenda for Council Meeting #2.

As you can see, this agenda introduces a number of new issues, some of which are more or less routine tasks that the Summerville City Council must attend to and some of which concern the future of the community as a whole. In addition to the new issues, the council must address the budget, knowing that it must be resolved before the end of Council Meeting #4.

You will want to review each of the issues that are on the agenda for this meeting to see if there are any direct or indirect relationships between the role or roles that you are playing and the issues. You should be particularly concerned about whether you need to make a presentation to council or whether you should be lobbying or trying to strike an alliance to achieve your objectives.

FIGURE 7.1 Agenda, Council Meeting #2

SUMMERVILLE CITY COUNCIL

Agenda
Council Chambers

1 **Call to Order**

2 **Approval of Agenda**

3 **Adoption of Minutes**—Council Meeting #1

4 **Introduction of Late Items**

5 **Public Hearings** (and third reading or adoption of by-laws where applicable)
   a) Beauty salon rezoning

6 **Delegations & Requests to Address Council**—Nil

7 **Report of Chief Administrative Officer**
   a) City Treasurer – Budget items for consideration by council
   b) City Administrator – Centrum Hotel and Casino

8 **Unfinished Business**

9 **Correspondence**
   a) Letter of complaint about the "Wild Flower House"
   b) Regional district re. fire protection
   c) Summerville Sash and Door

10 **Reports of Committees, COTW, and Commissions**—Nil

11 **Resolutions**—Nil

12 **By-laws**—Nil

13 **Question Period**

14 **New Business**

15 **Adjournment**

EIGHT

Subsequent Council Meetings

The agendas for each of the following meetings will be prepared by the City Clerk (in consultation with the Acting Mayor and the City Administrator) and will be made available to the participants. Your instructor will inform you about the issues that will be on the various agendas.

8.1   Council Meeting #3

As was the case with the previous council meetings, you will need to review the agenda to determine whether your character is involved in any way with the issues and what, if any, action should be taken. Members of council should be prepared to make substantive progress on resolving budget issues, at least to the extent of agreeing to an outline of a potential solution to the budget issue or to a narrowing of the issues that have to be resolved.

8.2   Council Meeting #4

The budget debate must be concluded by five minutes before the end of this meeting, and any decisions about tax or fee increases must be made by then as well.

8.3   Council Meeting #5

Any sitting member of the Summerville City Council who wants to run for mayor must announce her or his intention to run before the end of Council Meeting #5. Those who announce their intention to run for mayor are deemed to have resigned their positions on council, effective at the beginning of Council Meeting #7. Their positions on council will be open for election, and nominations from any member of the community will be received by the City Clerk up to the end of Council Meeting #6.

Any citizen of Summerville can run for mayor or for a position on council, and has until the end of Council Meeting #6 to submit nomination papers to the City Clerk.

8.4   Council Meeting #6

Any citizen of Summerville can run for mayor or for any position on council that may be vacant because the incumbent member of council has decided to run for mayor. The deadline for submission of nomination papers to the City Clerk is the end of Council Meeting #6.

8.5   Council Meeting #7

This council meeting will commence with the election of a mayor. If any members of council have resigned in order to stand for election as mayor, elections will also be held at Council Meeting #7 to fill the vacancies. The election will be held pursuant to the election legislation that is set out in Section 12.

8.6   Subsequent Council Meetings

The instructor will give you advice during Council Meeting #7 about the content of subsequent council meetings.

NINE
Summerville —A History

Summerville is a small town of 22,368 inhabitants that is located in the central part of the province of Cascadia. It is 150 km south of the City of Youngston (population 300,000) and 350 km west of the City of Churchill (population 500,000). The southern suburbs of Youngston, in particular Jackson (population 50,000) and Manchester (population 30,000), are just over an hour's drive from Summerville. Douglas, the capital of Cascadia, is located 600 km to the south of Summerville and has a population of 1.2 million.

9.1   Geography

Summerville is situated in a wide valley that runs generally in a north–south direction. The valley bottom is largely sandy loam and clay soils, and slopes gently from the east to the west. The Spring River meanders through on the west side of the valley, between one and two kilometres from the eastern valley walls. On the west side of the river, the valley walls rise sharply to the adjacent plateau. While the east side of the valley has relatively good soil and a gentle slope leading up to the east side's valley escarpment, the west side's steep hills, being close to the river, are unstable and prone to slippage, particularly when they become supersaturated after a series of heavy summer storms. At one time (prior to European settlement), there was a lake towards the north end of town. However, sedimentation and declining water levels have dramatically reduced its size.

In general, the river banks are stable, but geotechnical specialists have long warned the city that a major land slide on the west side of the river could result in a natural dam in the river, perhaps raising the river level by five or six feet before water is able to break through the loose dirt from the slide. The area of most concern is just downstream from Riverside Acres.

Flooding has not been a problem for many years, although there is some evidence that flooding was once a problem on the Spring River. It is believed that the diversion of water for agricultural purposes and the construction of some small-scale water storage dams have stabilized water flows. Nevertheless, engineers have speculated that, in the case of extreme rainfall lasting several days, water levels could rise by three or four feet, which would be enough to flood parts of Riverside Acres and the downtown area.

9.2   Early History

Summerville was first settled in the 1860s. The first settlement consisted of a roadhouse, stable, and small ranch. The founder, James Summer, purchased all the land in the river valley and developed a steady and modestly lucrative business that served travellers on the road between the provincial capital in the south and the gold fields north of Youngston. The main north–south road ran along the plateau on the east side of the valley, dipped down into the valley, and ran parallel to the river to a point just north of the slough, where the river could be forded. From there, the road climbed up the west bank of the valley and continued north. Summer's settlement, located on a high point adjacent to the river, presented a lovely summer oasis with its birch and cottonwood trees and grassy pastures. In the winter, the settlement was sheltered (at least relatively speaking) from the cold winds that blew across the plateau.

Within a decade, Summer had expanded his operation to include a general store that served the surrounding agricultural community. He had also established a small sawmill that he operated periodically to meet his and his neighbours' needs for lumber. By the turn of the century, the settlement had grown to include a small post office, a one-room school, and a dozen or so houses for his employees. By 1905, James Summer decided that he had grown weary of ranching and running his mini-conglomerate. He sold his holdings to Walter McGivney, a property and railroad developer. McGivney was involved with a consortium that was promoting a branch railway line that would

Summerville Road Network

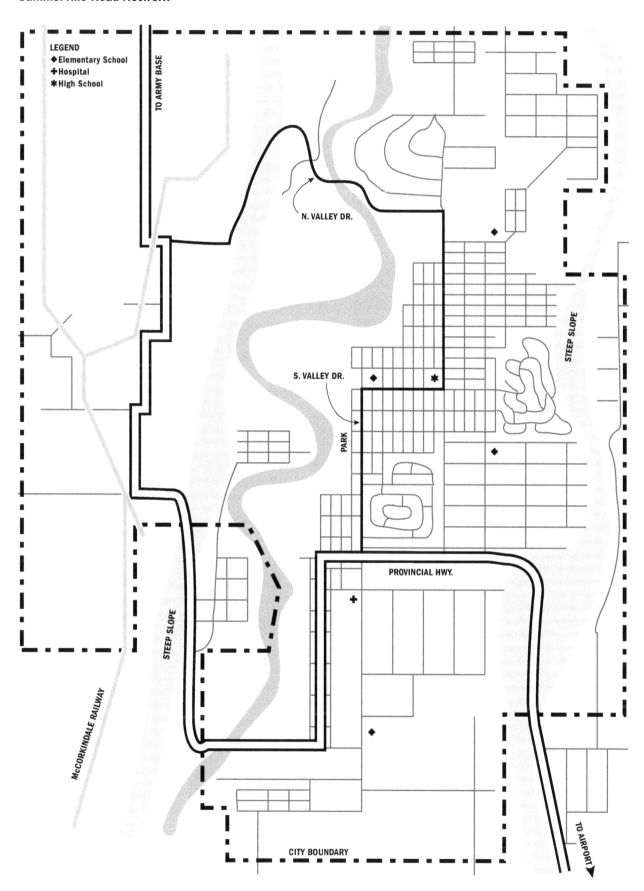

LEGEND
◆ Elementary School
✚ Hospital
✱ High School

TO ARMY BASE

N. VALLEY DR.

S. VALLEY DR.

PARK

STEEP SLOPE

STEEP SLOPE

McCORKINDALE RAILWAY

PROVINCIAL HWY.

TO AIRPORT

CITY BOUNDARY

run along the top of the west bank of the river. He took advantage of the coming of the railroad to expand the small community of Summerville. The ranch lands were subdivided into a series of 4-hectare parcels, which were heavily promoted as ideal sites for growing fruits and vegetables. A town site was subdivided, providing land for additional houses and businesses, adjacent to Summer's original roadhouse. The coming railway was to provide the means of moving the products to market. As part of his promotional package, McGivney developed a rudimentary water system (which drew water directly from the river) and constructed what he described as an "opera palace" but which was, in reality, little more than a community hall with a stage at one end and some rather garish decorations. A consummate promoter, McGivney was very successful and quickly sold the lands. Although he had indicated that he intended to take up land in the area, he quickly departed. It was rumoured that he was enjoying his profits in the San Francisco Bay area.

McGivney's operation was, in many ways, typical in an era when promoters used the promised railroad as a way of selling land to those who believed that the coming of the railroad would bring industry, residents, jobs, and wealth to those who moved to the new communities. It was, in one particular sense, atypical; a town was actually created, with residents and at least modestly profitable businesses. By the start of World War I, Summerville was home to about 525 residents. The railroad actually came in 1913, and provided a small amount of employment. More significantly, it provided a way of moving fruits and vegetables to market, as was originally envisaged.

At first, World War I resulted in a decline in population as many of Summerville's men volunteered for military service. The population recovered somewhat when a sawmill was constructed adjacent to the railroad tracks. The sawmill took advantage of the stands of good softwood in the surrounding area and of the wartime need for building materials. Not much happened in Summerville from 1918 until 1939. The population was more or less stagnant, and the economy was relatively unchanged. While the Great Depression was certainly felt by residents, its impact was not as dramatic or traumatic as it was in the larger cities. The railroad and the government continued to

provide a few steady jobs, and food was relatively cheap and plentiful.

The start of World War II brought rapid growth to Summerville. There were five major factors that led to an increase in population from 701 in 1936 to 5,716 in 1946. The need for building materials resulted in an expansion of sawmilling. The railroad's operations increased—creating a need for more employees—as it was used to move freight and personnel. Agricultural activity increased as the area became an important source of fruits, vegetables, milk, and meat for major military training bases located to the north and south of Summerville. About 10 kilometres north of Summerville, the army constructed a small base that was used to train army engineers. That base provided some employment opportunities for the town's residents. It also created customers for the town's hotels, restaurants, and bars. A small hospital was constructed to meet the health care needs of the army base and the community, which resulted in jobs for nurses, doctors, aides, and cleaning and kitchen staff. Finally, the growth in the community created a need for more schoolteachers, police, and trades people.

Most of the residents thought that the town would shrink after the end of World War II, as they expected the army base to close and the demand for lumber to decrease. In fact, the opposite occurred. The army base was maintained and converted into a training school for combat and field engineers. (It was eventually closed by the federal government in the 1990s.) This training school provided steady, direct employment for almost 100 people in Summerville. Lumber production increased, and the mills that had been built to serve the needs of the wartime economy remained in business and prospered. Truck loggers based their operations in Summerville, and there was growth in machine shops, equipment supply outfits, tire repair shops, and heavy-duty mechanical shops. Two major oil companies opened bulk plants to supply gasoline, diesel fuel, and lubricants to the logging and agricultural sectors. More people moved to Summerville, the schools expanded, and the number of retail merchants increased. Two department and mail order chains opened small retail stores in the downtown area. By 1955, the population of Summerville had increased to 8,230. Community leaders were

Summerville Land Forms and Major Features

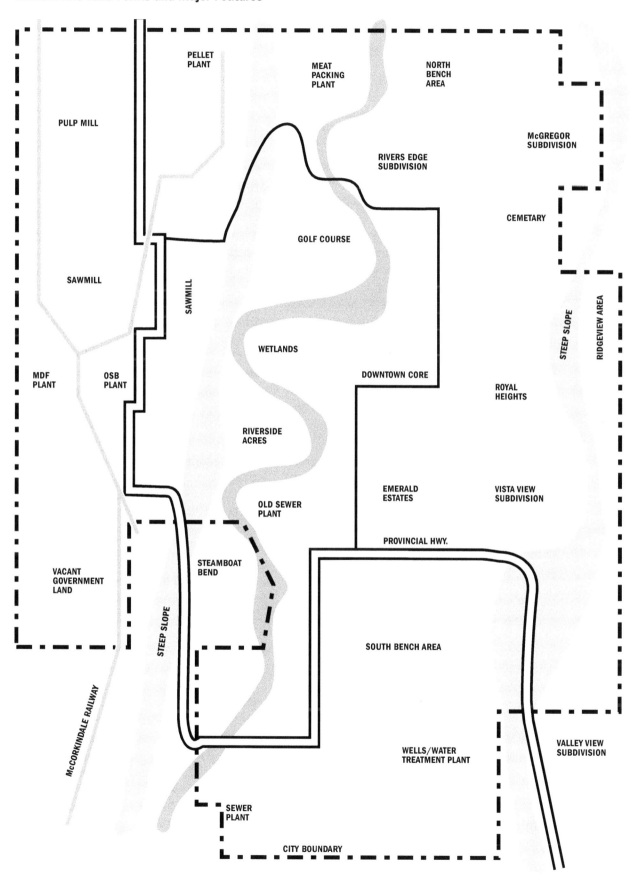

PULP MILL

PELLET PLANT

MEAT PACKING PLANT

NORTH BENCH AREA

McGREGOR SUBDIVISION

RIVERS EDGE SUBDIVISION

CEMETARY

SAWMILL

SAWMILL

GOLF COURSE

STEEP SLOPE

RIDGEVIEW AREA

MDF PLANT

OSB PLANT

WETLANDS

DOWNTOWN CORE

ROYAL HEIGHTS

RIVERSIDE ACRES

EMERALD ESTATES

VISTA VIEW SUBDIVISION

OLD SEWER PLANT

PROVINCIAL HWY.

VACANT GOVERNMENT LAND

STEAMBOAT BEND

STEEP SLOPE

SOUTH BENCH AREA

McCORKINDALE RAILWAY

WELLS/WATER TREATMENT PLANT

VALLEY VIEW SUBDIVISION

SEWER PLANT

CITY BOUNDARY

pleased with the rate of growth but believed that "the best was yet to come."

9.3   Industrial Development

In 1955, there were three major developments. In response to increased traffic on the north–south provincial highway, the province announced a major upgrading of the highway (completed in 1957). In Summerville, the upgrading included a new bridge across Spring River to the south of town and a new route up the escarpment on the west side of the valley. This meant that highway traffic no longer came down into the valley, through the town centre, across the old bridge north of the slough, and up the bank on the east side. Instead, it was able to go, at highway speeds, down into the valley, across the valley, and up to the plateau. Within two years of the new road's completion, developers had constructed a new motel and restaurant, a gas station, and a small hotel and pub at the intersection of the new highway and Valley Drive. Business at the two downtown hotels declined sharply to the point where they really were beer parlours that catered to a local clientele. The speed limit on the part of the highway that abuts the commercial development was reduced to 60 km/hr within three years of the highway's completion due to the number of traffic accidents.

The second major development was the construction of a small pulp mill. The mill, completed in 1960, significantly increased the scale of logging and the utilization of waste wood in the area. Nevertheless, the beehive burners at the four original sawmills were kept in operation to consume the large quantities of wood waste. The pollution generated by these burners maintained Summerville's reputation for having the worst air quality in Cascadia.

The third major development was the construction of an integrated meat packing plant, consisting of a feedlot, slaughterhouse, and a cutting and packaging facility. The plant created direct employment for about 150 people.

9.4   Maturity

By 1961, the population of Summerville had almost doubled to 15,483. The population continued to grow, albeit slowly, until it reached 23,415 in 1981. Summerville was expected to have a bright future. There had been concern that improvements in the provincial highways (which reduced the travel time between the major centres to the north, east, and south of Summerville) would lessen the demand for hotel and motel rooms, but the decline failed to materialize. The highway improvements had reduced travel time, but the road improvements had resulted in increased tourism. Summerville is close to the McCorkindale mountain range (to the southeast) and, as such, has served as a supply centre for hunting and fishing expeditions (and, more recently, eco and extreme tourism). The pulp mill, sawmills, the surrounding farms, and the meat packing facility were all profitable. The railroad's business was steadily increasing, bringing increased employment, but there were some concerns that the trucking industry might reduce railway usage. Few residents predicted the changes in Summerville's economy that began in 1981.

At first, hardly anyone noticed that there were fewer and fewer full time farms. Many of the farms had been converted into "hobby farms" or "estates" and no longer produced fruits and vegetables for the market. By about 1986, people said there were more horses than cows in the region. The decline in farming began to create problems for the meat packing plant. Not only was there a shortage of cows to be slaughtered but the plant was facing stiff competition from much larger integrated operations owned by multinational agricultural corporations. By the turn of the century, the only active part of the plant was a feedlot that was used to hold cattle until they could be shipped by truck to slaughterhouses in neighbouring Youngston and Churchill. Today, fewer fruits and vegetables move to market, and, as a consequence, employment in packing fruits and vegetables for shipment is significantly lower than it used to be.

Significant consolidation in the forest industry is also evident. There are now three sawmills, an MDF (medium density fibreboard) plant, an OSB (oriented strand board) plant, and the pulp mill. The logging and wood processing industry is effectively controlled by two large corporations. (One owns two sawmills and the MDF plant, and the other owns the pulp mill, the OSB plant, and one sawmill.) While the volume of wood processed has increased, growing productivity (the result of computerization and mechanization) has meant that

Province of CASCADIA

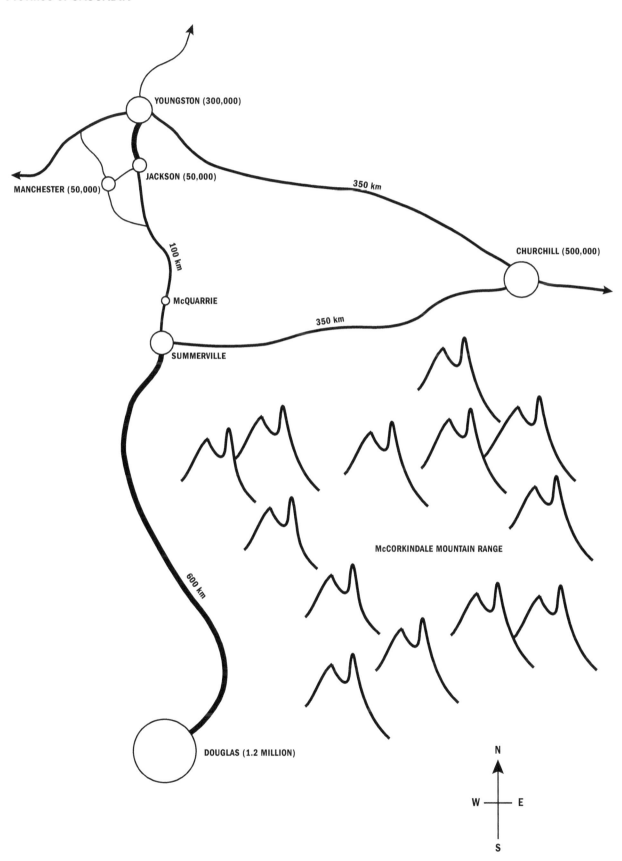

fewer employees are needed both in the woods and in the plants. Local interests, with corporate offices in Summerville, used to own the sawmills. Acquisition of the local sawmills by the integrated corporations has meant that local executive offices have been closed, and their administrative functions have been relocated to the corporate head offices in the provincial capital, Douglas.

Many of the forestry operations used to be carried out by crews employed by the sawmill companies or the forest tenure holders. In recent years, the companies have shifted to contracting the work out to independent logging and trucking contractors. Many of the contractors are based in Summerville, but some are from other communities and only come to Summerville during the times of the year when they can carry out operations in the woods.

Given the difficulties that the local economy has experienced in recent years, a number of residents have sought employment in the southern suburbs of neighbouring Youngston. The commute is about an hour in good weather, but the road can become treacherous in the winter, making travel difficult and dangerous.

9.5   Demographics

Over the years, the population of Summerville has gradually aged. As a result, there are fewer children, fewer classes, and fewer teachers. Budget constraints and changes in medical practices have resulted in about 25 per cent of the hospital beds being closed. More and more patients are referred to specialists in the nearby major cities. The centralization of government services has also meant that many local branches of federal and provincial government offices have been "downsized" or eliminated.

As a result of these trends, Summerville's population has declined to 22,368. (See Table 9.1 for a summary of population data.) Most of the households in Summerville consist of one or two people, although the average number of people per household is 2.5. (See Table 9.2 for household data.) About 53 per cent of the residents own their own home. Only 11 per cent of the owners spend 30 per cent or more of their household income on housing while 42 per cent of the renters spend more than 30 per cent of their household income on housing. About 85 per cent of the housing units were built prior to 1980. Only 5 per cent of the housing units are more than 50 years old.

The unemployment rate is 14.7 per cent. Unemployment is concentrated in the 15–24 age group, in which 24.5 per cent of the males and 27.2 per cent of the females are unemployed. Most people are employed in manufacturing, hospitality, retail, and health and social services industries, as shown in Table 9.3. The top eight occupations are sales and service; clerical; machine operations in manufacturing; labourers in processing; managers in retail, food, and other sales and service establishments; mechanics; and food/beverage service workers. These eight occupations account for about 40 per cent of all employed persons.

The relatively high level of unemployment is reflected in incomes in the community. Almost 14 per cent of total income comes from government transfers, and median personal income is relatively low compared to median incomes in the province

TABLE 9.1 Population Data

	TOTAL	MALE	FEMALE
Total Population	22,368	10,961	11,407
Population 15+ years	17,314	8,484	8,830
Single, Never Married	32%		
Legally Married	46%		
Separated	5%		
Divorced	10%		
Widowed	7%		
Never Married, Children Living at Home	7,290		
Average Number per Family	1.2		
Population Age Distribution			
0–4 years	6.3%		
5–19 years	24.8%		
20–44 years	39.5%		
45–64 years	19.2%		
65–74 years	5.5%		
74 years +	4.7%		
Seniors (65 +)	1,523		
Living Alone	48%		
Living with Family Members	52%		
Aboriginal Identity	382		
Visible Minorities	3,552		
Immigrants	3,579		
Population 15+ in Labour Force	11,292		
Unemployed	1,661		
Employed	9,632		

as a whole. Family income is also below provincial norms. Income data is shown in Table 9.4.

9.6   Land Uses

A visitor to Summerville who drives in from the south (which is the road to the airport) is greeted by the Valley View subdivision. Most people do not realize that this subdivision, a mix of single-family residences, mobile homes (both single and double wide), and small home-based business, lies outside the city boundaries. It was developed when the pulp mill was constructed. Valley View has a rudimentary private water system, septic tanks, gravel roads, and very low taxes. It appeals to people who prefer not to have to abide by many regulations and who are not bothered by their neighbours' more or less unregulated activities. The road to an area of smallholdings along the top of the ridge (imaginatively named "Ridgeview") runs through Valley View. A portion of Ridgeview is in the city (the result of negotiations by an aggressive council when the city boundary was extended to include Royal Heights). Properties in Ridgeview do not have any services, other than the gravel road, electricity, telephone, and natural gas. Ridgeview residents rely on private wells for their water.

Going down the hill from Valley View, the visitor can look over the south end of the city, known as the "South Bench Area." This is an area of relatively large lots (including some parcels that might be referred to as "hobby farms"). This area has very good soils, and, prior to the coming of the pulp mill, a number of fruit and vegetable farms existed here. A small subdivision, with city-sized lots, is located towards the southern city boundary (just north of the sewer treatment plant). That subdivision (which has yet to be named) has water and sanitary sewer services and paved roads. The rest of the south bench is served by the municipal water system, but there is no sewer. The roads are paved (as are virtually all the roads within the Summerville city limits).

When visitors reach the intersection of the provincial highway and Valley Drive, they must make a choice. If they continue ahead on the highway, they will come to a strip development of tourist or highway-oriented businesses. There is a hotel and pub, a motel, restaurant and bar, a motel without any food services, and two fast

TABLE 9.2 Household Data

PRIVATE HOUSEHOLDS	5,855
One Family	67%
Non Family	32%
Multi-Family	1%

FAMILY SIZE	
One Person	27%
Two Person	34%
Three Person	15%
Four/Five Person	20%

TABLE 9.3 Top Eight Industries by Labour Force

INDUSTRY	PERCENTAGE OF LABOUR FORCE
Manufacturing	22%
Accommodation, Food & Beverage	12%
Retail Trade	10%
Health, Social Services	8%
Construction	6%
Logging & Forestry	6%
Other Services	5%
Education	2%

TABLE 9.4 Income Data

	SUMMERVILLE	PROVINCE
Income from Employment	76.3%	75.8%
Income from Government Transfers	13.6%	11.8%
Income from Other Sources	10.10%	12.4%
Median Total Income	$19,521	$22,095
males	$28,565	$28,976
females	$14,513	$17,546
Average Family Income	$55,577	$64,821
couple families	$60,531	$70,033
male lone-parent families	$40,108	$47,480
female lone-parent families	$28,654	$33,829
Incidence of Low Income Population		
in private households	14.8%	17.8%
unattached individuals	34.6%	38.1%
Average Household Income	$50,399	$57,593
Median Household Income	$44,700	$46,802

food restaurants. At the very south end of the strip, there is also an old-fashioned steak-house that is a favourite haunt of truckers. (There are constant arguments about whether the food or the parking is the major attraction.) The highway then turns right and leads the visitor to the river, over a bridge, and up the escarpment to the upper level. As the visitor goes up the hill, the Steamboat Bend development is visible on the right.

Steamboat Bend is another residential sub-division outside the city boundaries. It is very similar to the Valley View area except that it has a proper water supply. The city provides water to the residents of Steamboat Bend under a contract to the regional authority. The provision of the water was a quid pro quo for the rights to get access through Steamboat Bend to provide water service to Riverside Acres. The city has made a number of attempts to have Steamboat Bend incorporated into the city, but the property owners have, so far, refused to approve an extension of the city boundary. There are those who say that the residents of Steamboat Bend will never approve a boundary expansion as long as they can enjoy most of the benefits of the city (such as use of recreation facilities and the library) without having to pay the taxes associated with those benefits. Steamboat Bend is one of the areas that developed quickly to house residents who were drawn to the area by the construction of the pulp mill. As far as it is known, the area's name is pure whimsy, as there is no recorded use of steamboats on the Spring River.

Just up river from Steamboat Bend is the small subdivision of Riverside Acres. This area was developed after World War II. Originally, access was by way of a one-way wooden bridge that linked Twelfth Avenue to Riverside Acres. The bridge collapsed in 1981, and the city decided that it was not economical to replace it. Instead, a road was constructed from the provincial highway through Steamboat Bend. Riverside Acres has a number of vacant lots. Soils are poor, and most of the lots cannot be served by septic tanks under current sewage disposal regulations. The area is not served by the city sewer system. The road between Riverside Acres and Steamboat Bend is hazardous in the winter. It is narrow, very close to the river bank, and subject to black ice and fog; the road has seen a number of close calls as drivers have, on several occasions, misjudged the corner and almost ended up in the river.

Continuing up the hill to the plateau, the visitor encounters a number of jogs in the main highway as it passes the pulp mill, the MDF and OSB plants, and the sawmills. The visitor would undoubtedly notice the large, cleared, empty site at the southwest corner of the city. The provincial government owns that site, and local rumour has it that the government is eager to sell it to a large multinational retail chain to be developed as a "big box" retail shopping centre. The circuitous route that the main highway takes in crossing from the east to the west plateau has been a topic of debate for some years. When the highway was built in the 1950s, residents saw it as a great improve-ment over the old route (which followed Valley Drive through what is now the downtown and then up to the west plateau at the north end of the valley). However, the increased use of trucks for hauling general merchandise as well as wood chips, logs, and lumber has caused a bottleneck for the trucking industry and a noise problem for the residents of South Bench (and, in fact, for the whole southern part of the city). Local residents and politicians have been pressing for some improvements for some time, but there is little agreement on the best way to improve the route. Both the local member of the provincial legislature and the province's highways authority openly favour a new four-lane road that would cross the Spring River south of the city and run along the eastern city boundary, completely avoid-ing the residential, commercial, and industrial developments in the valley. The town's access to the new highway would be in the vicinity of the crown land that may, or may not, be developed as a big box retail outlet. Needless to say, many busi-ness owners are not happy about that proposal, but many residents in the south end of the city look forward to its adoption, which would bring about a substantial reduction in noise levels.

If our visitors continue along the provincial highway, they will come to an intersection with the north end of Valley Drive. If they turn on to Valley Drive, they will go down a relatively steep hill (on a narrow, two-lane road) to the valley bottom. The city's golf course (operated by the Summerville Golf and Country Club) will be on the right, and the meat packing plant will be on the left. Visitors will cross the old, single-lane bridge (with traffic lights at each end) and come into the old part of Summerville. The North Bench, River's Edge, and McGregor subdivisions are to the north (along with the city's cemetery).

Summerville developed in four easily defined stages. The first stage (the initial town site created by Walter McGivney) consisted of 12 blocks of land around what is now the intersection of Valley Drive and Ninth Avenue and a large number of small farms to the north and south. A school (that provided schooling from grades one through nine) was constructed on a site at the corner of Ninth Avenue and Valley Drive (where the current elementary school now stands). During World War II, the network of rectangular blocks was extended north and south of the early development to provide housing to the government and lumber industry employees who were attracted to the community. The high school was constructed on a full four-block site on Ninth Avenue. The site provided playgrounds for the school, as well as sports fields for the community. In the 1950s, growth was accommodated by extending the residential areas and by subdividing many of the farms into smaller holdings suitable for use as hobby farms or rural estates. The Emerald Estates subdivision, incorporating new approaches such as cul-de-sacs and crescents, was created during this time to provide "high end" housing.

In the late 1950s and early 1960s, Royal Heights, Vista View, and the subdivisions north of the city centre were created to accommodate the rapidly increasing population. The high-density development in the centre of the community was fully serviced. The original water system was abandoned during World War II, and proper wells were dug and a modern (for the day) water supply system was installed. The system was expanded as more land was subdivided, but it was not extended beyond the central area until the city's boundaries were expanded in 1977.

The boundaries of the city have changed considerably over time. The first village was formed in 1927 with quite small boundaries. It was subsequently expanded twice to include more land, but the boundaries did not extend south of Fourteenth Avenue or north of First Avenue until 1955. At that time, the boundary was extended to include all the area on the west side of Spring River (so that all of the industrial development would be within the city's boundaries). It was also extended south along Valley Drive to the intersection of Valley Drive and the provincial highway. The area between Valley Drive and Spring River was included, as that was the site of the planned sewer treatment plant.

Sanitary sewers, serving only the high-density areas, were installed in 1955, and a sewage treatment plant was constructed on the banks of the river. The plant provided primary treatment only (screening of sewage and some aeration) and was located on the east side of the river, just upstream from Steamboat Bend.

By 1972, it had become evident that something needed to be done about the water supply for the areas that were still outside the city boundaries. In addition, the sewer treatment plant was overloaded and, at times, discharged more or less untreated sewage into the river. Furthermore, septic tanks were failing in many of the subdivisions that were not served by the sanitary sewer system (particularly the North Bench, McGregor and Vista View areas). By working together with the member of the legislative assembly and the province's department in charge of municipal affairs, the rural residents were able to develop a plan that called for expansion of the city's water supply to service the neighbourhoods to the south and north of the city with community water and to construct a new sewer treatment plant and sewer mains to service the North Bench, McGregor, River's Edge, and Vista View subdivisions, as well as the unnamed subdivision adjacent to the new sewer treatment plant site. The plan called for demolition of the old sewer treatment plant. In return for the extension of the water and sewer services, the residents agreed to an expansion of the city's boundaries. Despite significant lobbying, the residents of Steamboat Bend and Valley View would not agree to be incorporated into the city's boundaries. The boundary expansion (which included the South Bench, the North Bench, McGregor, River's Edge, and Vista View areas) took effect on January 1, 1977, and the construction of the sewer plan and sewer mains was complete by the fall of 1980.

The city's boundaries have remained unchanged since 1977. As noted earlier, there are periodically proposals to extend the boundaries to take in either Steamboat Bend or Valley View, but, because the residents of those areas are opposed (primarily because they already have access to most services they want and they feel that incorporation would bring only higher taxes), the proposed expansions have not succeeded.

TEN

Issues

The issues that may be placed before the Summerville City Council are discussed in this section. Not all the issues will be included in your simulation. Your instructor will choose which issues your city council will be asked to address. The intention is to allow the simulation's participants to explore and resolve the issues in their own way and, by doing so, to provide the experience of participating in the political process. Of course, this does not mean that there are no rules to follow. You and your colleagues must operate within the bounds of the law, council procedures, the norms of society, and the parameters established by the simulation.

10.1   Election of an Acting Mayor

The mayor, who was elected at the civic elections two years ago, was fatally injured in a traffic accident sixteen days before Council Meeting #1.

According to the Schedule of Acting Mayors for the City of Summerville, members of council share the mayoral responsibilities when the mayor is not available or temporarily incapacitated, with responsibilities being rotated among council members on a monthly basis. Councillor #3 has the responsibility for the current month and is responsible for chairing the first part of Council Meeting #1 (during which an acting mayor will be selected to replace the deceased mayor until the citizens of Summerville can elect a new mayor).

A by-election will be held to fill the vacant mayor's office. (At the previous meeting, council set the election date to be the day of Council Meeting #7; information on the election can be found in Section 12 of this workbook.) The election of an acting mayor will be the first item on the agenda at Council Meeting #1. It is known that some members of council have aspirations for higher office, and one of the factors they want to consider is whether serving as acting mayor would improve their political fortunes or not. A decision on who will be acting mayor cannot be deferred.

The election of an acting mayor is set out in the council's procedure by-law (Appendix 1). You will see that the procedure is relatively simple. Only the members of council can vote for the acting mayor. The acting mayor must already be a member of the city council. The person who is selected to be the acting mayor will immediately assume that responsibility, and will chair the balance of Council Meeting #1.

The Summerville Sentinel

Mayor Dies in Tragic Car Accident

By Guy Smiley

Long-time mayor of Summerville, Bob Russell, was killed last night when his car veered off Highway 7, just north of Summerville. Russell, who was alone in the car, was returning from a meeting in Youngston. He apparently lost control of his car and plummeted into a steep gorge just south of the village of McQuarrie. In recent years, a number of accidents along this stretch of Highway 7 have earned it

the infamous distinction of being the most dangerous road in Cascadia.

Russell was first elected mayor in 1998 and was reaching the end of his third term in office. It was expected that he would run for a fourth term, but he had made no public announcement of his intentions. Russell leaves his wife, Audrey, two children, and three grandchildren. Funeral arrangements are being coordinated by DeWiel and Sons, Funeral Directors.

TABLE 10.1 Budgeted Expenses Approved by Council in the Budget Discussions to Date ($ x 1,000)

	Last Year's Approved Budget	This Year's Preliminary Budget	Net Change Increase/ (Decrease)	% Increase / (Decrease)
General Operating (see Table 10.2)	41,139	41,697	558	1%
General Capital Expenses (see Table 10.6)	3,000	3,435	435	15%
Water Operating (see Table 10.3)	4,650	4,321	(329)	(7%)
Water Capital (see Table 10.6)	911	535	(376)	(41%)
Sewer Operating (see Table 10.4)	1,699	1,783	84	5%
Sewer Capital (see Table 10.6)	429	441	12	3%
Transit Operating (see Table 10.5)	708	869	161	23%

The by-election for mayor will be held at the beginning of Council Meeting #7. Any citizen of Summerville (any member of the class) can run for mayor. If members of council want to run for mayor, they must resign from office at the council meeting before nominations close (Council Meeting #5), and the by-election to fill the vacancies on council created by their resignations will be held at the same time as the by-election for mayor. Their resignations take effect at the beginning of Council Meeting #7. Any citizen of Summerville can run for the vacated positions on council. Council members who resign to run for mayor continue to be members of council until the election for mayor has been held. Nominations close just before the end of Council Meeting #6. The elections are held at the beginning of Council Meeting #7.

Members of the city's administration may also run for office, but they must first announce this intention and take a leave of absence from their administrative duties. Other members of the administration must be appointed to their positions temporarily.

10.2 Resolution of Congratulations

The Senior Girls Volleyball Team from Summerville Secondary School recently won the Provincial Girls High School Volleyball Championship (in the division that is reserved for medium-sized high schools). This is the first time that any team from Summerville has won the championship, although previous teams won the bronze medal nine years ago and the silver medal eighteen years ago. This recent success has caused a considerable "buzz" in Summerville.

Councillor #1 is very proud of the team's success; having a daughter on the team helps, but this is not the only reason for feeling satisfaction. Councillor #1 feels that events such as these build community spirit and add lustre to the city's reputation. Therefore, the councillor has given council notice of a motion of congratulations that will be presented at Council Meeting #1. The motion reads as follows:

"On behalf of the city's residents, the Council of the City of Summerville extends congratulations to the Senior Girls Volleyball Team for its resounding success in winning the Provincial Girls High School Volleyball Championship and for setting such a fine example of sportsmanship and accomplishment for the community."

10.3 Completing the Current Year Budget

The legislation governing municipal financial planning imposes a strict deadline for the adoption of the by-laws authorizing the budget and the imposition of taxes. Council has not been decisive, and a number of issues remain to be decided. It is imperative that the council adopts the budget and decides on tax and user charge increases (if any), by five minutes before the end of Council Meeting #4.

Council has reviewed and agreed to a great deal of the budget, but there are a number of unresolved issues. It has become very evident that there is simply not enough money to allow the city to undertake everything that people would like, unless taxes or user charges are increased or unless money is appropriated from the city's reserves. The budget items that have been agreed to are regarded as more or less "essential" by most of council. Total expenditures agreed to in the course of the budget discussions to date are shown in Table 10.1. You will see from Table 10.2 that, on the basis of discussions to date, there is $340,440 available to cover additional general expenditures. However, the total value of items that have been identified as desirable additions to the budget comprise $3,408,800. The items are listed and discussed in the following pages.

At Council Meeting #1, the City Treasurer will report to the council on the timetable for making decisions on the budget and on the budget issues that will be scheduled for discussion at Council Meeting #2. Council has no option but to deal with the budget issue, and must approve a balanced budget no later than five minutes before the end of Council Meeting #4, so the Treasurer will have time to prepare the budget by-law for Council Meeting #8. The council must also provide direction to staff about any increases that it wants to make in taxes or user charges by that deadline, so the city staff will have an adequate amount of time to prepare the necessary by-laws (which also must be ready by Council Meeting #8).

Before discussing the budget issues in detail, you may require some definition of terms.

First, in this simulation, we will talk about "**budgets.**" In many jurisdictions in Canada, provincial legislation requires that municipalities produce a "financial plan." A financial plan covers revenues and expenses, for both capital and operating purposes, for a period of not less than five years. The requirements for financial planning applicable to Summerville can be found in the legislative extracts section in Appendix 2. In this simulation, the term "budget" can be taken to mean "financial plan."

Second, local government officials often talk of "**capital expenditures**" and "**operating expenditures.**" The distinction is important because of the way in which the differing expenditures can be financed. "Capital expenditures" are expenditures for something that has a lifetime of more than a year, such as an office building, truck, bridge, park, or computer. Traditionally, capital expenditures are financed from current revenue, by borrowing (debt), by leasing, or by appropriating money from reserve funds. "Operating expenditures" are

expenditures for the current period. Examples would include the cost of salaries and benefits for staff, operating costs for buildings and equipment, materials and supplies used in the course of providing city services (e.g., paper, pens, consultants, and private contractors). Traditionally, operating expenditures must be financed from current revenue. In rare cases, however, it may be possible to finance operating expenditures from reserve funds.

There are some general principles of budget making that apply in this simulation, and in real life. They include the following:

1. The budget cannot provide for a deficit. Operating expenditures cannot exceed operating revenues, and debt cannot be incurred to finance operating expenditures. It is possible to appropriate money from "surplus" to cover current operating expenditures. Surpluses arise when operating revenues exceed operating expenditures. Every municipality likes to have some surplus (which is really the amount by which the municipality's financial assets exceed its liabilities) as it is the equivalent of the business corporation's "working capital." Similarly, the source of funding for capital expenditures must be at least equal to the capital expenditures. If debt is incurred, or if a lease is entered into, the term of the debt or the lease must be less than the anticipated useful life of the asset to be purchased (so that the ratepayers will not be put into the position of continuing to pay taxes for an asset that has been torn down or sold).

2. Budget proposals have to be realistic. All budget figures are estimates, and there is never any absolute guarantee that costs or revenues will equal the figures contained in the budget. However, they are realistic estimates. In other words, there should be a high probability that the estimated expenditures or revenues will be reasonably close to the amounts expressed in the budget. Budget proposals cannot be based on whim or "fancy." It is not probable that the city could win the lottery and resolve the budget problems, nor is it probable that a philanthropist will show up and offer to buy the sewer system for some grand sum. When reviewing any budget proposal, council should

TABLE 10.2 General Operating Budget Summary

	Last Year's Approved Budget	This Year's Preliminary Budget	Increase / (Decrease)	% Increase / (Decrease)
REVENUE				
Property Taxes	30,811,857	31,995,000	1,183,143	4%
Payments in Lieu of Taxes	3,488,664	4,038,747	550,083	16%
Fees and Charges	4,579,413	4,215,591	(363,822)	(8%)
Licences, Permits, and Fines	435,000	514,500	79,500	18%
Other Revenue	1,823,586	1,273,866	(549,720)	(30%)
Total Revenue	**41,138,520**	**42,037,704**	**899,184**	**2%**
EXPENDITURES				
Debt Servicing	930,228	2,628,549	1,698,321	183%
General Government	7,793,241	5,884,149	(1,909,092)	(25%)
Protection to Persons and Property	13,221,951	13,008,156	(213,795)	(2%)
Transportation (Public Works)	11,913,120	12,478,893	565,773	5%
Parks and Cultural Services	2,757,600	2,249,040	(508,560)	(18%)
Community Development Services	1,791,480	1,884,777	93,297	5%
Transfer to Transit Fund	467,400	588,510	121,110	26%
Transfer to Capital Equipment Replacement Reserve	67,500	78,000	10,500	16%
Transfer to Capital Infrastructure Reserve	111,000	227,190	116,190	105%
Transfer to Community Works Fund	435,000	435,000	–	–
Transfer to General Capital	1,500,000	1,935,000	435,000	29%
Transfers to Emergency Reserve	150,000	300,000	150,000	100%
Total Expenditures	**41,138,520**	**41,697,264**	**558,744**	**1%**
Preliminary Budget Funding Surplus		340,440		
Funding Surplus (Gap) as a % of Tax Levy		1.1%		

TABLE 10.3 Water Operating Budget Summary

	Last Year's Approved Budget	This Year's Preliminary Budget	Net Change Increase / (Decrease)	% Increase / (Decrease)
REVENUE				
Customer Billings	2,520,000	2,520,000	–	0%
Less: Discounts	(177,000)	(177,000)	–	0%
Connection Charges/Custom Works	45,000	45,000	–	0%
Water Availability Charges	54,000	54,000	–	0%
Provincial Government Grants	306,198	330,198	24,000	8%
Frontage Taxes	1,919,100	1,919,100	–	0%
Total Revenue	**4,667,298**	**4,691,298**	**24,000**	**0.5%**
EXPENSE				
Administration	714,270	621,978	(92,292)	(13%)
Distribution	754,650	865,500	110,850	15%
Pump Houses	616,500	641,550	25,050	4%
Hydrants	58,000	59,700	1,700	3%
Debt Servicing	1,595,973	1,596,573	600	0%
Transfer to Water Capital	910,500	535,500	(375,000)	(41%)
Total Expense	**4,649,893**	**4,320,801**	**(329,092)**	**(7%)**
Surplus	17,405	370,497	353,092	2,029%
Total (Expense and Surplus)	**4,667,298**	**4,691,298**	**24,000**	**0.5%**

consider whether a "reasonable person" could (or would) conclude that there is a "reasonable probability" that the revenues or expenditures will be close to the amount shown in the budget proposal.

3. The budget proposals must be within the law. The kinds of expenditures, taxes and fees and charges proposed in the budget must be the kinds permitted by the legislation applicable to Summerville.

4. The council can decide to increase taxes, user charges, permits, or fees. In all cases, the increases must be authorized by by-law (hence the need to meet the deadline for adoption of the budget so that the staff can prepare the necessary by-laws).

5. You cannot change the facts to suit your wishes. In real life, councils must take the facts as they find them (recession, failure of infrastructure, windfalls in revenue resulting from economic growth). They cannot change the world just because it does not satisfy their desires. Similarly, in this simulation, you cannot change the facts as presented in this workbook. You can interpret them however you want, but you cannot change the facts.

Thus, where cost and revenue estimates are given for the various budget issues, you must take them as they are. For example, in one of the budget issues it is stated that a police officer costs $97,600 per year per officer. You cannot decide that you will pay only $88,000. You can decide how many officers to hire, but each one will cost $97,600.

The general operating budget pays for core services such as public works, policing, fire protection, corporate and community services, and planning and development services. The revenues to pay for these services are comprised of property taxes, as well as fees for licences and permits, fines (including traffic fines), rental income, interest earnings on investments, and a variety of other revenues. The general operating budget is summarized in Table 10.2.

In addition to the general operating budget, the City of Summerville also has operating budgets for the water, sewer, and transit funds, and these are illustrated in tables 10.3 to 10.5. These three functions are treated as separate business entities. The water system operations are supported primarily through the city's water user charges. Due to a reduced capital program, an operating surplus of $370,000 is expected this year. The general operating budget for the water operating fund is shown in Table 10.3

TABLE 10.4 Sewer Operating Budget Summary

		Last Year's Approved Budget	This Year's Preliminary Budget	Net Change Increase / (Decrease)	% Increase / (Decrease)
REVENUE					
Customer Billings		854,000	938,000	84,000	10%
Less: Discounts		(56,000)	(66,000)	(10,000)	(18%)
Connection Charges/Custom Works		31,000	31,000	–	–
Provincial Government		96,800	96,800	–	–
Frontage Taxes		408,000	408,000	–	–
Transfer from Prior Year's Surplus		365,252	374,878	9,626	3%
	Total Revenue	**1,699,052**	**1,782,678**	**83,626**	**5%**
EXPENSE					
Administration		296,460	261,886	(34,574)	(12%)
Collection System		171,100	238,700	67,600	40%
Line Cleaning		92,700	95,300	2,600	3%
Treatment and Disposal		403,800	439,800	36,000	9%
Debt Servicing		305,992	305,992	–	–
Transfer to Sewer Capital		429,000	441,000	12,000	3%
	Total Expense	**1,699,052**	**1,782,678**	**83,626**	**5%**

The sewer utility operating budget summary is shown in Table 10.4. Unlike the water utility (which has an operating surplus), the sewer utility had an operating deficit last year. The budget provides for another deficit this year. At the end of last year, the accumulated prior year's surplus amounted to $340,000, which is insufficient to cover this year's projected deficit. A by-law was enacted early last year to increase the user fees by 10 per cent last year and by an additional 10 per cent this year. The additional revenue is incorporated into the projected revenues shown in Table 10.4. In order to avoid a deficit in the sewer operating fund this year, it is necessary to increase user fees, increase frontage taxes, or reduce expenditures. The budget that the council will adopt cannot include a deficit in the sewer fund.

The revenues and expenditures for the city's transit system are recorded in the transit system operating fund and are summarized in Table 10.5. The transit system provides a scheduled bus service throughout the community, as well as a special door-to-door transit system for the elderly and those with physical disabilities. The system is financed by transit fares and the general property tax. You will see that a significant increase in the contribution from the general operating fund is required for the next budget year. This is the result of a decision last year to expand the transit service to provide more hours of operations and better routes to meet the needs of students and seniors.

Capital expenditures, and the sources of funding, are summarized in Table 10.6. Summerville's financial plan is shown in Table 10.7.

As indicated above, there are a number of expenditures that councillors would like to undertake, if they can find an acceptable way of financing the costs. Here are items that council wishes to consider:

1. COUNCIL TRAVEL COSTS—The existing budget is only enough to allow half of council to attend the annual convention of municipal leaders and for the mayor to make six trips to the capital city. The recently deceased mayor wanted an extra $25,000 to allow all members of council to attend the convention and so that the mayor could go to the capital at least once a month to lobby the government.

2. STAFF TRAINING—The existing budget provides 0.25 per cent of salary and wage costs for staff training and professional development. The Administrator has expressed considerable concern that this is insufficient to allow staff to keep pace with changes in technology, legislation, and management issues. In addition, it does not provide for the employment of any apprentices, and the city is having trouble finding certified mechanics and pipe fitters. Increases in training costs have meant suspending the policy of paying for courses that lead to professional certification. The Administrator has requested that the staff training budget be increased to 1 per cent of

TABLE 10.5 Transit Operating Budget Summary

	Last Year's Approved Budget	This Year's Preliminary Budget	Net Change Increase / (Decrease)	% Increase / (Decrease)
REVENUE				
Transit Fares	216,600	259,500	42,900	20%
Advertising Revenue	12,000	9,000	(3,000)	(25%)
Transfer from General Operating Fund	467,400	588,510	121,110	26%
Misc. Revenue	12,000	12,000	–	–
Total Revenue	**708,000**	**869,010**	**161,010**	**23%**
EXPENSES				
Administration	18,000	15,600	(2,400)	(13%)
Transit Operations Contract	597,000	699,300	102,300	17%
Other Expenses	93,000	154,110	61,110	66%
Total Expenses	**708,000**	**869,010**	**161,010**	**23%**

TABLE 10.6 Capital Expenditures

	Last Year's Approved Budget	This Year's Preliminary Budget	Net Change Increase / (Decrease)
GENERAL			
General Expenditures	**3,000,000**	**3,435,000**	**435,000**
Funded by:			
General Operating	1,500,000	1,935,000	435,000
Community Works Fund	278,422	162,900	(115,522)
Debt	1,221,578		(1,221,578)
Capital Equipment Replacement Reserve		63,900	63,900
Capital Infrastructure Replacement Reserve		178,800	178,800
Land Sales Reserve		1,094,400	1,094,400
Total Funding for General Expenditures	**3,000,000**	**3,435,000**	**435,000**
WATER			
Water Expenditures	910,500	535,500	(375,000)
Funded by:			
Water Operating Fund	910,500	535,500	(375,000)
SEWER			
Sewer Expenditures	429,000	441,000	12,000
Funded by:			
Sewer Operating Fund	429,000	441,000	12,000

salary and wage costs, which would mean a total cost of $106,000 per year.

3. BUILDING INSPECTION—Presently, the budget means that one of the two building inspectors has to be laid off during the months of November through March (when there is little building). This short-term layoff was proposed as a means of reducing the budget. In order to avoid the lay-off, the city could increase the fees for building permits by 35 per cent, as that would produce sufficient additional revenue ($36,000) to cover the cost of keeping the inspector employed. Summerville's building fees are slightly lower than the average for municipalities of similar size in Cascadia. A building permit for a $50,000 project costs $450 in Summerville, compared to $460 in the average municipality (fees across the province range from $400 to $775). Plumbing permit fees in Summerville are comparable to the average elsewhere ($60, plus $8 per fixture, with a minimum of $70). The city's objective is to have the fees for building and plumbing permits cover the costs of inspection. In years when construction activity is strong, the fees more than cover the cost of providing the inspection service. However, in years when there is relatively little new construction (as is the case this year), the fee revenue does not cover the cost.

4. FIRE DEPARTMENT—The pick-up truck that the fire chief uses is now four years old. The chief has requested a new vehicle (at a cost of $37,000), noting that his truck now has 83,000 kilometres. He also points out that this vehicle lacks four-wheel drive. The City Administrator has already advised council that a four-wheel drive vehicle is not needed. (Summerville seldom gets deep snowfalls, and the chief has not been able to show that he has ever been stuck.) Also, the Administrator feels that a compact car (costing $17,000) would be adequate, as the chief does not use the truck to carry equipment.

5. FIRE DEPARTMENT—The chief has asked that an additional fire fighter be added to the department to reduce the amount of overtime that is used by the department. In the first year, the cost of this addition would be $21,000, but the cost would rise to $87,000 the following year. A copy of the chief's report to council on this addition can be found in Figure 10.2.

TABLE 10.7 Financial Plan

			YEAR 1 (LAST YEAR)	YEAR 2 (THIS YEAR)	YEAR 3	YEAR 4	YEAR 5
General Operating	*Expenses*	Debt Servicing	930	2,629	2,232	2,058	1,913
		Other Purposes	37,477	35,845	36,920	37,659	38,412
		Expenses Sub-Total	38,407	38,474	39,152	39,717	40,325
	Transfers to Reserves Funds:	Emergency	150	300	300	300	300
		Community Works	435	435	435	435	435
		Capital Infrastructure	111	227	232	237	241
		Equipment Replacement	68	78	78	78	78
		Sub-Total	764	1,040	1,045	1,050	1,054
	Transfers to Other Funds:	Capital Fund	1,500	1,935	1,974	2,013	2,053
		Transit Fund	468	589	601	613	625
		Sub-Total	1,968	2,524	2,575	2,626	2,678
		Transfers Sub-Total	2,732	3,564	3,620	3,676	3,682
		Total Expenses and Transfers	**41,139**	**42,038**	**42,772**	**43,393**	**44,057**
	Funded by	Property Value Taxes	30,812	31,995	32,875	33,298	33,760
		Fees	4,579	4,216	4,300	4,386	4,474
		Other Sources	5,748	5,487	5,597	5,709	5,823
		Total Funding	**41,139**	**41,698**	**42,772**	**43,393**	**44,057**
		Surplus (Deficit)	–	340	–	–	–
General Capital Expenses		**General Capital Expenses**	**3,000**	**3,435**	**3,074**	**3,013**	**3,253**
	Funded by	General Operating Fund	1,500	1,935	1,974	2,013	2,053
		Debt	1,222				488
		Community Works Fund	278	163	153	325	65
		Capital Equipment Reserve		64	55	90	35
		Capital Infrastructure Reserve		179	120	165	
		Land Sales Reserve		1,094	772	420	612
		Total Funding	**3,000**	**3,435**	**3,074**	**3,013**	**3,253**
Water Operating	*Expenses*	Debt Servicing	1,596	1,597	1,488	1,462	1,112
		Transfer to Water Capital	911	535	295	715	316
		Other Expenses	2,142	2,189	2,211	2,255	2,323
		Total Expenses	**4,649**	**4,321**	**3,994**	**4,432**	**3,751**
	Funded by	Frontage Taxes	1,919	1,919	1,919	1,919	1,919
		Fees	2,442	2,442	2,442	2,445	2,471
		Accumulated Surplus				68	
		Other Sources	306	330	330		
		Total Funding	**4,667**	**4,691**	**4,691**	**4,432**	**4,390**
		Surplus (Deficit)	18	370	697	-	639
Water Capital	*Expenses*	Water Capital Expenses	911	535	295	715	316
	Funded by	Water Operating	911	535	295	715	316
Sewer Operating	*Expenses*	Debt Servicing	306	306	306	306	
		Transfer to Sewer Capital	429	441	18	3	204
		Other Expenses	964	1,036	1,057	1,067	1,089
		Total Expenses	**1,699**	**1,783**	**1,381**	**1,386**	**1,293**
	Funded by	Frontage Taxes	408	408	408	408	408
		Fees	829	872	876	881	885
		Accumulated Surplus	365	340			
		Other Sources	97	97	97	97	
		Total Funding	**1,699**	**1,717**	**1,381**	**1,386**	**1,293**
		Surplus (Deficit)		-66			
Sewer Capital	*Expenses*	Sewer Capital Expenses	429	441	387	812	242
	Funded by	Water Operating	429	441	17	3	204
		Land Sales Reserve			100	200	38
		Debt			270	609	
		Total Funding	**429**	**441**	**387**	**812**	**242**

6. FIRE DEPARTMENT—The fire department has asked for 18 sets of facemasks and breathing equipment. The existing equipment (some of which is only two years old) has been rendered obsolete by new provincial occupational health and safety regulations. The city must meet the new regulations by April 1 of the next year. Each set of equipment (which includes facemask, regulator, mouthpiece, tank, and attachments) will cost $3,700. The Treasurer has suggested that the equipment could be ordered late this year for delivery early in the following year, as that would allow the city to comply with the regulations and finance the cost out of next year's budget. The Fire Fighters' Union has written a letter to the City Administrator protesting this proposal and seeking an audience with the Summerville City Council (see the letter in Figure 10.3).

7. POLICE—The police chief has requested that an additional officer be added to the department, effective July 1. The annual cost would be $97,600. The chief has indicated that Summerville's police department is understaffed compared to those of other municipalities. Summerville's crime rate of 263 criminal code offences per 1,000 population is quite high compared to the provincial average of 125. An analysis of crime statistics indicates that Summerville's incidence of crimes against persons is slightly above the provincial average, that crimes against property are significantly less than the provincial average, and that "other" types of crimes are higher than average ("other" includes offences such as prostitution, gaming and betting, weapons, arson, bail violations, disturbing the peace, and vandalism). Summerville's police force of 32 members averages 137 cases per officer, compared to a provincial average of 111. Provincial statistics for the previous year show that Summerville spent $241 per capita on policing services, compared to a provincial average of $153.

8. POLICE—A recent inspection of the police headquarters has revealed that the interview rooms do not meet federal standards for the protection of privacy. Specifically, as a result of decisions by the courts, it has been determined that, to comply with the Charter of Rights and Freedoms, a police department must provide a place where the accused can meet with his or her lawyer in private. The level of soundproofing in the existing interview rooms is well short of federal standards. In addition, the cellblock provisions for the separation of male and female juvenile prisoners do not meet federal standards. As a result, extensive renovations to the cellblock and prisoner booking areas are required. The cellblock renovations are expected to cost $85,000, while the renovations to provide proper interview rooms are expected to cost $125,000. These interview room renovations will take workspace away from the general investigation squad, and a small addition to the east side of the police station (costing $165,000) will be required, unless only the cellblock renovations are made.

9. EMERGENCY PROGRAM—The coordinator of the city's emergency measures program has told the City Administrator that the volunteer search and rescue team is in urgent need of a new van to carry equipment. A new van would cost about $48,000, but volunteers have found a five-year-old used unit that they can purchase for $8,000. The Administrator has expressed some concern about buying such an old vehicle, although it has only 63,000 kilometres.

10. LIBRARY—The existing budget provides a grant to the library that is 3 per cent higher than last year's grant. The Library Board (an autonomous board appointed by council that operates under the provincial Library Act and is responsible for all aspects of the library's operations) has expressed concern that, with the increasing cost of books, magazines, CDs, and DVDs, the budget is inadequate. Also, the budget does not allow the library to extend its hours so that it is open every evening, instead of just two evenings a week. The Library Board wants a $25,000 increase in its budget. Summerville's library is currently open to the public for 42 hours per week (10:00 a.m. to 5 p.m. on Tuesdays, Thursdays, and Saturdays and 10:00 a.m. to 8:30 p.m. on Wednesdays and Fridays). Provincial statistics indicate that,

FIGURE 10.2

1212 Main Street
Summerville

To: His Worship the Mayor and Council
From: Fire Chief
Subject: Additional Fire fighters

I have submitted a budget request for an additional fire fighter, at a cost of $21,000 for the current year. This fire fighter would be available to cover planned absences, so that we can meet our minimum staffing requirements without calling employees in to work at overtime rates. At present, when fire fighters go on vacation, are engaged on union business, or have other planned absences (such as training), we often have to pay overtime rates so that we have sufficient staff on duty. In the last fiscal year, the cost of this overtime was $118,612.

Having an additional fire fighter available would not eliminate overtime costs, as unplanned absences (such as illness-related time off) often necessitate calling in fire fighters to work on short notice. We do not know how much of the overtime is the result of unplanned absences.

If there are any questions, please let me know.

Respectfully submitted,
Fire Chief

on average, public libraries in the province are open 48 hours per week. Summerville's library receives $29.62 per capita from the city's budget, which is less than the provincial average of $33.22 per capita.

11. YOUTH CENTRE—A variety of proponents have suggested that the city open a youth centre to provide a place where teenagers could "hang out" with adult supervision and organized activities. They have calculated that, once fully operational, such a centre would cost $218,000 per year to pay for staff, rent, and operating costs. The proponents believe that they could get donations to cover about one-quarter of the costs, but they have no firm commitments. They want to be fully operational next year and need "seed money" to get the project going. They have asked for $61,200.

12. ARENA—The Zamboni is 23 years old, and the engine is failing. The Administrator has advised council that it will cost $218,000 to replace the Zamboni. It could be reconditioned for $25,000, but the existing natural gas engine gives off carbon monoxide, which is a known hazard in arenas. This item has been on the budget "wish list" for the past three years. There has been the odd time when the Zamboni hasn't been available to clear ice at the arena due to mechanical problems. Arena staff members admit that the unit would probably get through the next year as it has through the last three years, but replacement (or refurbishing) is inevitable. Meanwhile, the minor hockey association and the figure skating club maintain that a new Zamboni is essential to their bids to host provincial and regional tournaments.

13. SUMMER PLAYGROUND PROGRAM—In previous years, the city provided a free summer playground program for children aged five to twelve. Last year, the program cost $18,000 to operate for the summer, and a grant from the provincial government covered $12,000 of the cost. The grant is no longer available. The program generally attracted about 15 children per day.

14. DITCH CLEANING—The city's policy has been to have a ditch-cleaning program every three years. The last program was three summers ago. This program involves clearing sediment and growth from the drainage ditches alongside the rural roads. The estimated cost of cleaning all the ditches (outside the downtown core) is $112,500. If the ditches are not cleaned, it is possible that a major rainfall could produce more runoff than the ditches can handle, causing flooding to adjoining properties (for which the city might be held liable). The city has not had such flooding problems for several years (perhaps because of the ditch-cleaning program). Under questioning by council, the City Administrator indicated that the areas of major concern are Riverside Acres and the River's Edge subdivision and, to a lesser degree, Vista View. Ditches in these areas constitute about a third of the total number to be cleared. A review of the records shows that, the last time there was flooding, the interval between cleaning was five years and that flooding only occurred in the three areas mentioned above. There are no laws requiring that the ditches be cleaned, but the city is liable for damages if it is negligent in maintaining the storm drainage system.

15. PAVING—The city tries to repave some streets each year. The budget for repaving for the past five years has been $900,000 per annum, and this amount is included in the current budget. However, it is becoming evident that the city is not keeping up with the need to repave the roads. Potholes are increasing in size and number, and the citizens are complaining. The public works department has asked that the budget be doubled. This part of the budget provides for repaving where the pavement has deteriorated. It does not cover the construction of new roads, the paving of existing gravel roads, or the upgrading of roads and streets. Those costs are budgeted separately. The average life of a paved major street is 10 to 15 years (depending on soil conditions and the amount of traffic) while residential streets last from 20 to 25 years. Many of Summerville's residential streets were paved when the mills were constructed and have not been repaved since that time. Residents complain that their residential

FIGURE 10.3

SUMMERVILLE LOCAL 38 FIRE FIGHTERS' UNION

Mayor and Council
City of Summerville

Dear Sirs:

It was with considerable shock that the employees of your fire department learned that
your management staff wishes to defer the acquisition of facemasks and breathing
equipment until next year. While the legal requirements may allow you to defer the
purchase, the fact remains that the provincial government has determined that the
existing masks are unsafe and are hazardous to our members. In our view, your
administration is playing with our health and safety simply to meet artificial financial
targets.

The argument that the equipment is in good shape and has been trouble free for the
past five years is not sufficient reason to defer the purchase. Occupational health and
safety standards have decreed that new, improved equipment must be provided by
April of next year. Since the equipment is readily available, we believe that it should be
provided immediately to protect the health of your employees.

We hereby request an opportunity to appear before council as soon as possible so
that we may explain to you the importance of replacing the facemasks and breathing
equipment at the earliest possible moment.

Yours truly,
President,
Summerville Local Fire Fighters' Union

streets are becoming narrower as the pavement breaks away at the edges. Some municipalities have undertaken pavement management programs, which identify the scope of the problem and set out a plan of action. Summerville has not done that.

16. BACKHOE—The city's eight-year-old backhoe has become quite unreliable. While repairs have not been terribly expensive, the down time has resulted in crews sitting around waiting for the equipment to be repaired. There have been delays in responding to water main breaks, and, in one instance, a ditch across Valley Drive had to be left open for three days until the unit was fixed. Public works has asked that the unit be replaced (at a cost of $164,200), as replacement is overdue under the city's equipment replacement policy.

17. FLOWER BASKETS—The city has always had a program to hang flower baskets along the highway by the South Bench and along Valley Drive. This program costs $21,000.

18. ARENA HOURS—The Recreation Commission has requested that four hours per day be added to the arena operating hours during the winter months. Commissioners estimate that this will cost an additional $35,000 per year (the incremental costs are mainly for labour and utilities). In their view, these additional hours will give the minor hockey teams about 10 per cent more ice time, which should be advantageous to the "rep" teams. They believe that this expenditure can be financed in part by a 10 per cent increase in hockey fees (which would raise $6,000). The city would be expected to pay the rest of the cost.

19. GOLF COURSE—Under the city's agreement with the Summerville Golf and Country Club (the operator of the golf course), the club is responsible for maintaining the grass along the side of Valley Drive and for keeping the drainage ditches around the golf course clear. Last year, the club failed to keep the ditches clean and experienced some minor flooding of the 5th, 7th, and 10th fairways, as well as of the 9th green. Also, the club's standard of grass maintenance was poor, resulting in

a number of public complaints. The club's executives claim that they don't have the extra $3,000 to pay for this work and have asked that the city take on the responsibility, as the golf club is a major recreational amenity for the community.

20. WATER TESTING FEES—The provincial government used to provide free testing of water samples. The city must take three samples every week to ensure that the water supply is not contaminated. Each test costs $80 to process. This expense is not included in the budget.

The list of budget additions does not include the installation of sewers in Riverside Acres, a project that the city has been considering for a number of years now. A moratorium on the issuance of building permits for Riverside Acres was put in place a number of years ago because the water table and soils make the area unsuitable for the use of septic tanks. There are 42 lots in Riverside Acres, and only 17 are built on. The other 27 lots must remain vacant until sewers are installed. It is estimated that it will cost $622,000 to construct a sewer line from Riverside Acres, through Steamboat Bend, and across the highway bridge to connect with the existing trunk sewer main that will carry the sewage to the treatment plant. A lift station, costing $225,000, will be required, and it will cost $18,000 per lot to construct the sewer collection mains in Riverside Acres.

The medical health officer writes to council each year pleading for the installation of the sewer system in Riverside Acres, but successive councils have tabled the issue because of the relatively high cost. Therefore, the city administration has not included the project in the list of budget additions.

The taxable assessed values in Summerville for the current year increased by 5.4 per cent to $1,245,072,000. Increases were not uniform in all classes. Residential assessed values increased 6.5 per cent, major industrial assessments increased 1 per cent, and business assessments increased 6.6 per cent. In earlier discussions, council decided to leave the tax rates unchanged. Applying last year's tax rates to the current assessments results in a 3 per cent increase in property tax revenue. New construction (of houses, businesses, and industrial

TABLE 10.8 Taxes on a Representative House Last Year

School Taxes	$570
Municipal General	$489
Other Governments (regional and provincial taxing agencies)	$276
Parcel Taxes	$520
Total	**$1,855**

TABLE 10.9 Reserve Fund Balances at the End of Last Year

Name/Purpose	Balance
Water Treatment Reserve (for expansion of the treatment plant)	$451,212
Tax Rate Stabilization Reserve	$1,347,600
Rental Renovations Reserve	$832,000
Land Sale Reserve	$3,272,101
Tax Sale Reserve	$3,812
Landfill Closure Reserve (covering and sealing the landfill when it is full)	1,258,600
Community Works Fund	190,000
Capital Equipment Replacement Reserve	$277,913
Emergency Reserve	$2,142,000
Capital Infrastructure Replacement Reserve	490,766
Total	**$10,266,004**

buildings) has added about 1 per cent to the tax revenues. The implication is that the average property owner will experience a 2 per cent increase in her or his property tax bill. In previous discussions, council had determined that this level of increase was acceptable because it was in line with inflation. However, some members of council had pressed for a higher increase because they felt that city services would suffer if the tax increase were too low. Each 1 per cent increase in average taxation will give the city additional revenue of $203,300.

The total tax bill for a representative (typical) house in Summerville (valued at $192,404) is shown in Table 10.8. In addition, homeowners pay user charges for water, sewers, and garbage collection.

Parcel taxes are taxes that are imposed on property to finance the construction and maintenance of the water and sewer systems. They are levied on the basis of the size of the parcel, on the basis of frontage, or as a flat amount (i.e., $50 per parcel).

The city had $10,266,004 in reserve funds at the end of last year. This money has been set aside for a variety of purposes (listed in Table 10.9). The Tax Rate Stabilization Reserve was established to provide a fund that could be used to pay refunds to taxpayers if they are successful in obtaining reductions in the assessed value of their properties. Taxpayer appeals of assessed values can take years to resolve and, when the final decision is made, the city may be required to refund quite large amounts of previously collected taxes. The city has determined that a reserve equal to 10 per cent of the annual tax levy is desirable (but not always attainable).

The Rental Renovation Reserve is used to accumulate funds that can be used to finance renovations for tenants in city-owned buildings (funds are required from time to time to make renovations to the buildings to meet tenant demands). The Emergency Reserve was established to provide money that could be used to deal with the costs of one-time emergencies (such as unusual floods or forest fires). The target level for this reserve is 15 per cent of the general operating budget. The Land Sale and Tax Sale Reserves hold money that was obtained by selling city-owned land. The money in the reserves can be used for any capital purpose.

The Capital Equipment Replacement Reserve is intended to finance equipment required by the Summerville Public Works Department. The Capital Infrastructure Replacement Reserve was created last year with the intent to build a reserve to finance the replacement of water, sewer, storm sewer, roads, and recreational facilities when they reach the end of their economic life. The Landfill Closure Reserve contains money that has to be set aside, under the terms of the landfill licence, to close the landfill site properly when it is full, to prevent leaching and erosion, and to provide appropriate landscaping of the landfill site. The Community Works Fund was set up to provide a source of money for projects that would enhance neighbourhoods within Summerville.

10.4 Water Treatment Plant

The equipment used to chlorinate the water has become quite unreliable, and the equipment distributor has advised the public works department that, due to the age of the equipment, parts are becoming hard to get. The last time the equipment failed it took three weeks to get replacement parts. Fortunately, the city was able to borrow a replacement part from neighbouring Youngston,

FIGURE 10.4

Summerville
GAY PRIDE DAY COMMITTEE

Your Worship the Mayor
City of Summerville

Dear Mayor Russell:

Once again, the Summerville Gay Pride Day Committee requests that the city declare
Gay Pride Day and authorize a parade from the high school grounds to Riverside
Park. Since you have approved this request for the last six years, I am sure that I do not
need to explain the issue to you at great length. We are not proposing any change to
the event this year.

I will, of course, be available at the council meeting to answer any questions that you
or members of the Summerville City Council might have.

Yours truly,

Pat Rizzotto
Co-Chair,
Summerville Gay Pride Day Committee

which meant that the "boil water" advisory only lasted three days.

The city's consulting engineer has recommended that the entire filtration and chlorination system be replaced at a cost of $1,285,000. This expenditure would bring the system up to the standards required by new provincial legislation. Compliance with the legislation is required within three years. The consulting engineer has admitted, however, that the city could temporarily replace the chlorination equipment (at a cost of $212,300). The replacement equipment would restore operational reliability. However, it would not be compatible with the new filtration system that will have to be installed three years from now.

There are currently no provincial grant programs that could be used to assist the city in meeting the cost of the new equipment. Councillor #3 and Councillor #5 are of the opinion that, because there are a number of municipalities that must upgrade their treatment facilities and because there is a provincial election expected in the next two years, there is a good chance that the government will introduce a grant program as part of its election platform. There is, of course, no guarantee that this will happen or, if it does happen, that Summerville will be eligible for a grant under the program.

If Summerville is to do anything to resolve the issue this year, the matter must be decided in time to be included in the current year's budget. Consequently, a source of funding, and any related increases in fees or taxes, will have to be decided by the end of Council Meeting #4. Council has asked that the city's administrative team make recommendations in sufficient time to allow council to include the project in the current year's budget, if that is council's wish.

10.5   Gay Pride Day Resolution

The city has received a request from the Summerville Gay Pride Day Committee for a resolution declaring Gay Pride Day and authorizing a parade from the secondary school grounds to Riverside Park (see Figure 10.4). The request has been approved every year with little comment. The declaration of "days" and "weeks" (and even "months") to celebrate various groups and events has no legal meaning. It is simply a way of calling attention to something that is important to some group of citizens. However, declarations

FIGURE 10.5

The Hazards of Denying a Request for a Municipal Proclamation

In some provinces, municipal proclamations are considered a "service" that cannot be denied because of the colour, race, ancestry, place of origin, religion, marital status, family status, physical or mental disability, or sex or sexual orientation of that person or class of persons. A refusal to make proclamations requested by organizations representing minority groups may be contrary to human rights legislation. In some instances, tribunals have ordered that the municipality pay compensation when requests have been denied.

Changing the wording of the requested proclamation may also be considered to be discrimination, if changing the wording is not done for other requests.

have taken on great symbolism, and council needs to be careful that it does not discriminate when considering such requests.

10.6   Financial Support for Girls' Volleyball

Supporters of female sports in Summerville have been agitating for some time because they feel female sports receive less support than male sports. Until recently, their efforts have been directed toward the Summerville Board of School Trustees, as that board has provided money for a variety of primarily male school teams. However, two years ago, the provincial government reduced funding to school boards, and the school board reacted by reducing virtually all of its support to school teams. As a result, parents were required to meet the cost of transporting their children to out-of-town sporting events.

The supporters of the Senior Girls Volleyball Team at Summerville Secondary School have been negotiating with city staff for over six months to obtain some financial assistance. They have pointed out that the city provides significant subsidies for minor hockey and minor baseball. It is true that girl's softball receives free use of ball diamonds (as does the Summerville Little League and other youth baseball leagues, which are male-only leagues). However, they like to point out that there is only one softball diamond, which has to be shared by adults and youth, while there are five other ball diamonds, which are fully booked by male leagues. The only sport that appears to have achieved gender equity is the local soccer organization.

The group seeking financial support for the girls' volleyball team is led by the Sports Parent. This individual is very concerned about the lack of support for school teams (for both boys and girls) and wants to use the success of the girls' team to get the city involved in funding youth teams. The Senior Girls Volleyball Team is the only "success story" among local youth sports group. The boys' teams are rarely competitive, despite the amount of money made available to them, and the minor hockey and baseball programs have been mediocre, at best. There is no empirical evidence to indicate that the relative success or failure of the teams is related to funding. It may be that the Senior Girls Volleyball Team has a very good coach (but there is no evidence to prove that point either).

The Sports Parent has done considerable research, and here are the results:

» It costs the city $85/hour to operate the arena, but the city charges the minor hockey league $40/hour for non-prime time and $50/hour for prime time. (Minor hockey has all the prime ice time.)

» Figure skating has 15 per cent of the non-prime time and pays $40/hour.

» Minor hockey has 60 per cent of the non-prime time, and adult hockey has 25 per cent of the non-prime time.

» There are six ball diamonds, but only one is set up for softball. The city does not keep detailed records of the cost of maintaining the ball diamonds, but most people think that the softball diamond is actually maintained to a higher standard. (The parks foreman has said that this is because the men that use the other ball diamonds are prepared to do some of the maintenance of these diamonds on a volunteer basis and are prepared to accept lower standards of maintenance.)

The City Administrator discussed this issue with council at an *in camera* (private) meeting, expressing concern that the school board may be attempting to shift costs away from its budget to the city's budget and that this reduction in support may be the thin edge of the wedge. Also, the Administrator has reminded council that the city does not provide subsidies to any other teams. So far, the city has only provided facilities for youth sports and has not been involved in providing money for items such as coaching, travel, or uniforms.

The Sports Parent has made an appointment to appear before the council to attempt to convince councillors that they should include funds in the current year's budget to purchase uniforms and provide travel costs for the Senior Girls Volleyball Team. The Sports Parent has in mind a figure of $25,000 but has not really substantiated the costs.

10.7   Beauty Salon Rezoning

The Beautician is a single mother. Her husband was killed in an industrial accident last year, leaving her with a five-year-old son and a three-year-old daughter. Fortunately, their house mortgage was insured, so she is able to continue living in the family home (which is in the Vista View subdivision), but, as is the case with many young couples, the rest of their family finances were in very poor shape. As a consequence, she has very little income to provide for food and clothing. Prior to her marriage, she had worked in a beauty salon. She has renewed her beautician's license, and she opened a beauty salon in her basement recreation room about four months ago. The city quickly heard of the operation. City staff notified her that Vista View was zoned "rural residential" and that the zoning does not allow home occupations that bring customers to the premises. Thus, the Beautician was informed that she could not continue to operate the business from her home. She was, of course, quite concerned for two reasons. She did not want to get into legal difficulties. Second, having a beauty salon in her basement was a perfect fit for her situation; it allowed her to be in the house to supervise her children (thereby avoiding the expense of day care). Having her children at home is particularly important because she believes that her son may have learning difficulties and would benefit from more parental support than he would get if he were in day care. City officials indicated that they could not recommend rezoning. City policy requires customer-oriented service businesses to locate in the commercial areas. They did, however, advise her that she had a right to apply to council to rezone her property to

FIGURE 10.6

Summerville City Planning Consultants
1328 Main Street, Suite 912, Summerville

To: The Mayor and Council
From: Consultant Planner
Subject: Beautician's Rezoning Application

An application has been received to rezone a house in Vista View subdivision to allow the operation of a beauty salon in the basement of the house. Current zoning regulations do not allow home occupations that attract customers to the premises. Council directed that this matter be submitted to a public hearing and has given first reading to the required rezoning by-law. The by-law would change the zoning regulations so that home occupations that attract customers to the premises will be allowed provided that there is no exterior signage that indicates the presence of the business, provided that there are no employees other than the owner of the house, and provided that there are three off-street parking spaces.

City staff is opposed to this application because customer-oriented business should be located in the central business district. The downtown core will be weakened if such businesses are dispersed throughout the city. In addition, the public wants to preserve the purely rural nature of our beautiful subdivisions.

It is acknowledged that an alternative approach would be to "spot zone" this property to allow the proposed business. "Spot zoning" involves the creation of a zone in the zoning by-law that applies to only one or a very few properties. It is regarded as poor planning practice. If the property were to be "spot zoned," we would have to create a special by-law, advertise it, and send notice of the rezoning to adjoining properties, as well as hold another public hearing. We estimate that an additional five to six months would be required for this process.

Respectfully submitted,

City Planning Consultant

allow a home occupation that attracted customers to the premises.

She filed the application for rezoning (paying the $350 fee that the city imposes on such applications). Over three months ago, the council received the application and a staff report recommending against the rezoning, and directed that the application be the subject of a public hearing. The matter is now scheduled for a public hearing. The staff report recommending against the application is shown in Figure 10.6. That report will be entered into the record at the public hearing.

The Beautician has canvassed her neighbours and has found that, of the eight who live reasonably close, three are very supportive of her effort to operate a beauty salon and become self-sustaining, three do not care, and two are quite opposed because they fear that others will want to open customer-oriented businesses in the neighbourhood. They are afraid that traffic will increase, bringing more noise and hazards for their children. The Beautician has agreed that she will not have any signs that indicate the presence of the business in her house. She expects that most of her customers will be friends and close neighbours and is therefore reluctant to agree not to work on Sundays or in the evenings when her children are sleeping.

Councillor #1 is convinced that "spot zoning" is appropriate because it would allow council more control over retail operations in the rural residential zone. Councillor #3 supports more generalized zoning, believing that no harm would come from the proposed change to the rural residential zoning.

A public hearing on a zoning application is a very formal proceeding. It is classed as being "quasi-judicial," which means that the principles of natural justice have to be observed. The hearing must be conducted in a way that allows everyone who has an interest in the matter to be heard. All people must be given the chance to inform council of their opinions without being heckled, harassed, or intimidated by the audience. The applicant must be afforded an opportunity to hear what others are saying about the application and must be given a chance to rebut the presentations made against the application. The hearing opens with the City Clerk stating the nature of the application and the zoning change that is under consideration. That information is outlined in the staff report in Figure 10.6. If the role of City Planner has been filled, that person will present the information to council. If the role of City Planner has not been filled, the City Clerk will present the information that has been obtained from other staff members and from the city's consultant planner (who will not be present at the hearing). The applicant is then given an opportunity to outline the application and present any supporting information that the applicant feels the council should have. Then, anyone else who feels that his or her interests are affected by the proposed by-law that is the subject of the hearing is afforded an opportunity to make a presentation to council. When all interests have been heard, the applicant is allowed to make a summary statement. This summary is an opportunity to rebut any information that has been presented by others during the course of the hearing.

When all interested parties have been heard, a member of council will move that "the hearing be closed." If the motion is seconded (and adopted by council), the hearing will be closed, and the council may not receive any more information with respect to the application (although closing the hearing does not preclude council from asking technical questions of staff). Council then proceeds to debate the question of whether the by-law (which would give effect to the rezoning) should be adopted or not. Only members of council participate in that debate. The public, the applicant, and the staff are observers.

There is no requirement that council make a decision "on the spot." Councillors can delay a decision, but, if they do, they must be very careful to make sure that, between the close of the hearing and the time that they make a decision, they do not allow themselves to be "lobbied" on the matter and do not receive any information in addition to that which was presented at the hearing. If they are lobbied, or if they get new information, someone who is disappointed with the ultimate decision of council may be able to go to court and get this decision declared "null and void" because of a flaw in the hearing process.

10.8 Centrum Hotel and Casino

The town's largest firm of real estate agents (represented by the Real Estate Agent) has submitted a proposal to council for the development of a hotel and casino at the intersection of Ninth Avenue and Valley Drive, between Valley Drive and Riverside Park. The proposed casino hotel has been given the name "Centrum Hotel and Casino." It would comprise a 35-room hotel, a restaurant, a bar, and a casino with 125 slot machines, 25 gaming tables, and a bingo hall. The idea is to attract local residents as well as highway travellers and customers from neighbouring cities such as Youngston and even Churchill. The project would take up the whole block, and parts of Riverside Park (behind the development) would be taken for parking. Riverside Anglican Church, as well as a number of other heritage buildings, would have to be demolished or relocated to make way for the development.

The Real Estate Agent is acting on behalf of a syndicate from the provincial capital that has built four other casino hotels in the province and has a track record of establishing very profitable operations. There are few, if any, complaints about the way in which they operate their casinos, other than generic complaints about the negative effects of gambling. The proponents believe that there is a strong market for this product, and that the casino hotel will generate 250 new jobs within a year of completion. They also believe that there is a market for a convention and conference centre attached to the casino hotel, and they have indicated their willingness to operate such a facility should the city want to construct one. The developers have options to purchase all of the private land in the block. They have not obtained an option to purchase Riverside Anglican Church or the three lots that the city owns in the block. They have suggested to city staff that the city should assist them in negotiations with the church, noting that the city could expropriate the church property to facilitate the development. They have asked that the city name a price for its property.

The Real Estate Agent is assisted in this matter by the Casino Developer (if someone has been assigned to play that role).

The syndicate wants that particular site because of the vistas that it has to the north and east. (Riverside Acres is shielded from view by groves of large cottonwood trees.) The developers also believe that the elementary school (which is quite old) will be closed within the next few years, and they see an opportunity to acquire that site and part of the existing park, which could accommo-

FIGURE 10.7

The Summerville Sentinel

Historic Buildings Threatened By Casino Development

By Walter Plunkett

The proposed Centrum Casino and Hotel may be one of the most significant changes in the downtown core for many years, but, in the opinion of one local historian, the development poses a threat to some of Summerville's oldest buildings. According to the Chair of the Summerville Historical Society, Pat McGregor, if the casino project is approved, four historic buildings, including the Riverside Anglican Church, the McGivney House, the old library building, and another building that housed the first general store in Summerville, will have to be relocated. All of these buildings date from the turn of the century and, in the opinion of McGregor, are priceless parts of the city's heritage. The oldest is the Riverside Anglican Church, which was originally constructed in 1882 and is one of the oldest churches in northern Cascadia. The local real estate agency that is developing the property on behalf of Centrum Casino and Hotel, Incorporated, has assured city council that every precaution will be taken to preserve these historic buildings. However, McGregor said that, given the fragile state of the buildings, relocation to another site might not be possible. McGregor is particularly concerned about the church, one of only a few remaining original examples of nineteenth-century log construction in Cascadia. At a public meeting of the Summerville Historical Society yesterday, McGregor said that relocation would effectively mean demolition because the church could not withstand the move. The relocation of a similar log church in Youngston two years ago was not successful and resulted in the eventual demolition of the structure.

FIGURE 10.8

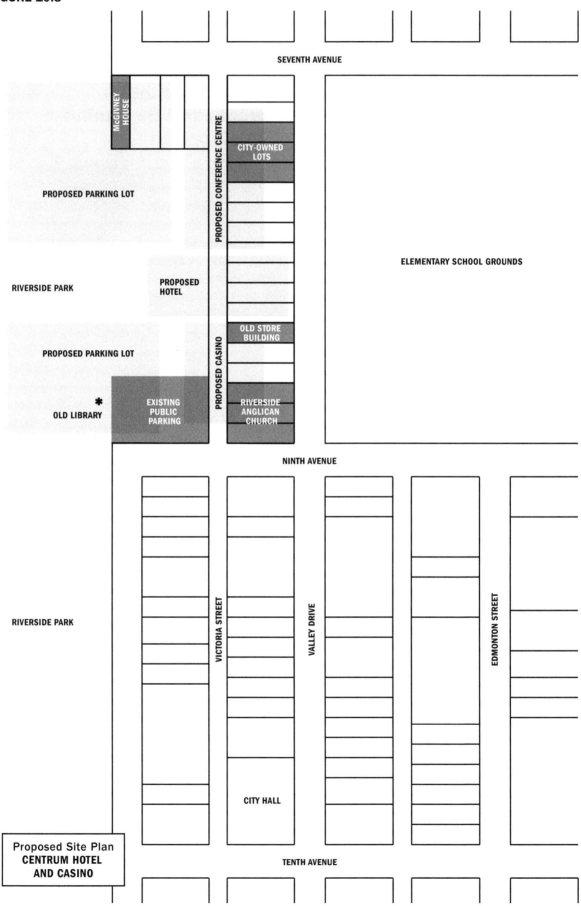

Proposed Site Plan
**CENTRUM HOTEL
AND CASINO**

date a much larger resort facility. They are aware that the city owns most of the next block to the south of their chosen site and that they could build there, but they feel doing so is not as suitable for their short- and long-term interests.

The parkland is used mainly by residents for walking their dogs and as an unsupervised and unstructured children's play area. It was part of the original Summer farm, and it was the location of many of the first buildings in Summerville. Some people, including members of the Recreation Commission, believe that the park could be developed into an outdoor recreational and tourist feature for the community.

In discussions with the City Administrator, the Real Estate Agent has indicated that the principals are aware of the proposal to relocate the highway to bypass the south bench and to build "big box" retail premises at the top of the hill. They believe that their proposal will not be viable if the highway is moved. They know that council has no control over the highway decision, but they are sure that, if council can give their project approval in principle within six weeks of Council Meeting #2, they can convince the province not to relocate the highway. They are aware that council will be holding a public hearing at Council Meeting #5 on the possible rezoning of land for "big box" retail outlets on the highway. That hearing is, by coincidence, six weeks away.

A map showing the proposed development is shown in Figure 10.8.

The Real Estate Agent has also suggested to the City Administrator that it is reasonable to expect that this project would have a dramatic impact on land prices all along Valley Drive. There would be increased opportunities for restaurants and other support services. If the "big box" stores are approved and the highway is relocated, and the casino project does not proceed, it is probable that "the downtown will wither on the vine." In addition, under provincial legislation, the city will receive a share of the gambling "take." It is estimated that the city's share would amount to about $500,000 in the first full year of operation.

The City Administrator received this application five days ago, and this is the first opportunity for the council to be made aware of the proposal. No one has had an opportunity to examine it in any detail. Council's first opportunity to discuss the issue will be at Council Meeting #2.

The City Administrator has written a report to council requesting direction and suggesting both that council should indicate what information it would like to have about the development and that it should arrange a meeting with the developer for Council Meeting #3. The Administrator has also suggested that, in advance of meeting the developer, councillors should begin to think about and discuss the kinds of constraints and conditions that they might want to impose on such a development. The development, according to the Administrator's report, would truly change the nature of the community, so all aspects of the matter have to be considered carefully. The City Administrator has strongly suggested that no decision be made until a public information meeting has been held. The earliest date for such a meeting would be Council Meeting #4.

10.9 Summerville Sash and Door

Summerville Sash and Door bid on the window replacement job for the city hall renovations. The company submitted a bid of $86,512. It was found to comply with all the specifications of the tender. However, Summerville Sash and Door was the second-lowest bidder. Another firm, from Youngston, submitted a bid of $85,712.50. The bid documents indicated that the city would "not necessarily accept the lowest or any bidder." The owner of Summerville Sash and Door (the Door Maker, Role 22) is incensed, has written a letter to council (Figure 10.9), and wants to speak to council about the matter.

The Door Maker did not, however, make any arrangement with the City Clerk to appear before council. He simply submitted the letter to the Clerk.

10.10 Regional Government Fire Protection

The city has received a letter from the regional government asking if Summerville is interested in entering into a service agreement with the regional government to provide fire protection services to Steamboat Bend. Steamboat Bend has had several opportunities to be incorporated into the city. The property owners in Steamboat Bend have indicated that they have no desire for city regulations and services. They were, however, successful in

FIGURE 10.9

**Summerville
Sash & Door**

1352 Pine Street
Summerville

The Mayor and Council
City of Summerville

Dear Mayor and Councillors:

I am writing to protest the award of the contract for new windows for the
Summerville City Hall to a supplier from Douglas on the grounds that the other
company bid lower than I did. The difference between our bids was $799.50, which is
less than half of the amount that I pay in taxes to the city each year. Your staff told
me that they have to take the low bidder to get the "best bang for the buck." Don't
they realize that if they had awarded the contract to me I would have employed four
local men for a month each to make and install the windows? The money that they
earned would be circulated throughout the community. The money that I earned
would have been spent on supplies and on paying my city taxes. Why don't you people
realize that?

It is not too late to correct your error. Cancel the contract with the big city carpet-
baggers and give it to someone who has supported the Summerville economy for
years.

I will be coming to your council meeting to get your decision.

Yours truly,

Summerville Sash and Door

FIGURE 10.10

The Summerville Sentinel

Fire Destroys House in Steamboat Bend

By Delilah Chan

A late-night fire in Steamboat Bend destroyed a house and left two children injured and in serious condition at the Summerville General Hospital. The cause of the fire was not known, but it is rumoured to have been the result of human error. City fire crews were unable to respond to the fire because Steamboat Bend is located outside city limits. When asked to comment, the Summerville Fire Chief simply stated, "City fire crews are not insured to respond to fires outside the city limits." Despite numerous previous attempts to incorporate Steamboat Bend into the City of Summerville, the residents of the neighbourhood have resisted.

Last night, these same residents reacted angrily to the fire department's decision not to respond to the fire. Becky Fortune, who has lived in Steamboat Bend for the last 20 years and has been active in the Neighbourhood Association Against Amalgamation (NAAA), the local group that opposes the incorporation of the neighbourhood into the city, said that the actions of the Summerville Fire Department were "criminally negligent." Unnamed sources at the department also expressed misgivings about the decision. One fire fighter said, "I have children of my own, so you can imagine that I wasn't too happy when I heard that children were at risk in the Steamboat Bend fire." Fortune has

requested a meeting with city officials to discuss the situation and is hopeful that some kind of resolution can be reached whereby fire services could be provided to the neighbourhood without requiring it to become part of Summerville.

negotiating to have the city provide potable water. That arrangement came about when the city found it had to construct a road between Riverside Acres and Steamboat Bend, and install a water main at the edge of that road, to serve the residents of Riverside Acres. The city had to construct the road and the water main because the old wooden bridge between the downtown and Riverside Acres had collapsed. The water main that served Riverside Acres ran across the old bridge.

A delegation of property owners in Steamboat Bend approached the regional government asking that fire protection services be arranged. A recent house fire in Steamboat Bend, which almost resulted in the death of two children, had shown them the value of having fire protection. Here are the facts of the matter:

» The city's fire department has one fire hall, located in the core of the city. If there is a fire on the east bench or in Riverside Acres, the city's fire trucks pass by Steamboat Bend on the way to the fire. Steamboat Bend is completely accessible to the fire department.

» Providing fire protection to Steamboat Bend will not add to the city's operating costs.

» The city faces substantial liability if its fire department attends a fire outside the city boundary. For example, if a house within city boundaries caught fire and was destroyed because a fire outside the city delayed the fire department's response, the owner of the house might be able to claim damages against the city for negligence. For that reason, the city has had a firm policy of not allowing the fire department to attend fires outside the city boundary. This liability issue would be less of a problem if there were a service agreement between the city and the regional government for the provision of fire protection to Steamboat Bend.

» The fire department personnel (regular and volunteer fire fighters) feel that they have a moral obligation to attend fires outside the city boundary if lives are in danger. They were very upset when the fire chief would not allow

TABLE 10.10 Fire Protection Data

	Steamboat Bend	City of Summerville
Single Family Dwellings	21	3,922
Assessed Value—Total	$1,785,000	$1,245,072,000
Average Taxes Paid by a Homeowner	$1,335	$1,855

them to take city fire trucks to the recent fire in Steamboat Bend.

Table 10.10 provides comparative data on the number of houses in Steamboat Bend and in Summerville, the assessed value of property in Steamboat Bend and in the city, and the average taxes paid by a homeowner in Steamboat Bend and in the city.

Council must decide whether it wants to enter into negotiations with the regional government to provide fire protection to Steamboat Bend and, if so, what general directions should be given to the members of the city administration who will negotiate the agreement with the regional government.

10.11 The "Wild Flower House"

The council has received a letter of complaint from four residents of Royal Heights concerning a neighbour who has ripped out the front lawn at her house and planted wild flowers. The letter is shown in Figure 10.11. The Wild Flower Lady has approached Councillor #4, asking that she be allowed to defend herself at the council meeting. Councillor #4 has told her that she probably will not be allowed to speak at the meeting during which the letter of complaint will be considered. The Wild Flower Lady, after consulting the City Clerk, is in the process of preparing a letter that she would like to read at the next council meeting (Council Meeting #3) defending her actions.

The issue before council is whether or not to direct staff to prepare amendments to the city's by-laws that would make it illegal to do what the Wild Flower Lady has done. Councillor #4 is particularly concerned about this issue. A long-time resident of Emerald Estates (which is similar to Royal Heights in many ways), this councillor particularly values the broad sweep of green front lawns, unbroken by fences, hedges, or other obstructions, and the manicured shrubs and care-fully tended formal flower-beds. This individual regards the apparently unorganized and unkempt profusion of wild flowers that has grown up in Royal Heights as an abomination.

10.12 Riverside Acres Building Permit

The owner of a vacant lot in Riverside Acres (Riverside Acres Owner) has approached the City Administrator requesting that a building permit be issued to allow construction of a single-family dwelling on a vacant lot. The house would be served by a septic tank. The city has imposed a moratorium on the issuance of building permits for new buildings in Riverside Acres because of the lack of a sanitary sewer system. The property owner claims to want to build while interest rates are low.

The City Administrator reluctantly agreed to put the question to council, even though quite sure that council would reject the request. Both the Administrator and the property owner know that council cannot order the issuance of a build-ing permit unless the health authority has issued a permit for sewage disposal. The health authority will not issue a sewage disposal permit in Riverside Acres. The health authority's medical officer insists that the city should install a proper sewer system in Riverside Acres.

10.13 Trade Mission to India

The Acting Mayor received an invitation from the Premier's Office to represent Summerville on a trade mission to India. The mission would take three weeks, and the cost to the city would be $13,000. The premier is taking three cabinet ministers, two deputy ministers, three aides, five other mayors, and eight heads of forest industry firms on the mission.

The Acting Mayor is very flattered to have been invited, and believes that the trip would be good for Summerville. Therefore, in a verbal report to council, the Acting Mayor will ask that coun-cil approve the expenditure (which would mean adding $13,000 to the budget). The Premier's Office wants to be advised not later than noon of the day following Council Meeting #3 whether the Acting Mayor will go.

FIGURE 10.11

Wolfgang Smith

1352 Elm Street, Royal Heights, Summerville

Mayor and Council of Summerville

Your Excellencies:

We, the undersigned four residents of Royal Heights, wish to draw your attention to the state of the yard of one of the residents of Royal Heights. The "Wild Flower Lady" (as we call her) has ripped out beautiful gardens and planted what can only be described as a weed patch of native flowers and shrubs. We think that this will detract from property values. We ask that you enact by-laws that will require residents to maintain neat, manicured lawns. With our abundant water supplies and good climate, there is no reason why all of our houses cannot be graced with lush green lawns.

Yours truly,
Four Residents of Royal Heights

FIGURE 10.12

The Summerville Sentinel

Letters to the Editor

Dear Editor:

Once again, it seems that the powers to be are contemplating an extravagant junket to Asia in the name of economic development, when they really should be paying more attention to what is actually going on in Summerville. While the mayor is off enjoying 3 weeks of exotic travel in India, the residents of Summerville must contend with flooding, dirty drinking water, and potholes so big they can swallow up a small car. If the mayor and council are interested in encouraging economic development in this city, they should focus their attention and resources on the problems at hand, not on expensive foreign travel that offers no guarantee of results.

Yours Sincerely,
Dudley C. Milquetoast

10.14 Wedding Shop Issue

The request for the beauty shop prompted another resident to ask for permission to run a wedding shop from the basement of a family home. The distinguishing factors here are that the shop is not yet in operation, and it will attract a lot of traffic, but the neighbours are supportive. This resident has asked to be represented by the Solicitor. The Solicitor has submitted an application for rezoning. It will be presented to city council by the City Planner. Councillors will have to determine whether they are prepared to consider the application and allow it to go to public hearing.

The house is located one block away from the main commercial area. It is in a predominantly residential area, but the neighbourhood could easily begin to transform into a commercial area if there were a demand for commercial real estate. The vacancy rate in retail premises in the downtown area is approaching 25 per cent, and the Real Estate Agent is concerned that approval of an application such as this could mean that businesses might vacate existing commercial buildings to relocate to houses on the fringe of the commercial area. The Real Estate Agent has several investments in the commercial area and, being experienced in the rezoning process, realizes that effective lobbying may keep the issue from ever going to a public hearing.

10.15 The "Too Big" House

The Building Contractor purchased an older home in the downtown area, about a block away from the secondary school. He purchased it intending to use the building as his family home, to accommodate his wife and three young children. Shortly after purchasing the house, he applied for a building permit to allow for extensive renovations. The plans showed that the attached garage was to be converted to a family room, and the existing kitchen and eating nook were to be extensively renovated. The renovation also involved a four-metre wide extension on the side of the house to provide for a master bedroom with bathroom on the first floor and two additional bedrooms on the second floor. The Building Inspector approved the plans, since the building, as designed, complied with the zoning by-laws.

When the foundations were poured and the Building Inspector was called to do the inspection, the fact that the addition was larger than indicated in the plans that accompanied the application for the building permit was noticed immediately. The four-metre addition was actually five metres wide. The addition, as originally proposed, did not encroach on the side yard, but it now appeared that the side yard would be reduced to 1.5 metres. The zoning by-law requires a two-metre side yard. In addition, the footings that had been poured for a new front porch were too close to the front property line, and a foundation had been poured for a garage that was not even shown on the original permit application. The Building Inspector immediately ordered the Building Contractor to stop work. After discussions, the Building Contractor agreed to redo the foundations for the addition to the house and not to construct the front porch. The Building Inspector agreed to add the garage to the approved building permit, since doing so complied with the zoning by-law. (The Building Inspector was given to understand that it would be a normal two-car garage.)

Because of a combination of time off and illness the Building Inspector was unable to visit the site again for three weeks (and the other building inspector was away on vacation). Upon

Figure 10.13

SUMMERVILLE CITY COUNCIL

City of Summerville
Skating Rink Fee Increase By-law
8872

The Council of the City of Summerville hereby enacts that:

1) Section 7 of Summerville Rates and Charges By-law No. 8866, 2005, is hereby repealed and the following is substituted therefore:

1) The admission fees charged for public skating shall be:
   a) For adults — $3.65
   b) For senior citizens — $2.10
   c) For "moms and kids" — $2.10
   d) For teens — $3.15
   e) For children — $1.05

2) This by-law may be cited as "Skating Rink Fee Increase By-law 8872 "

READ A FIRST TIME THIS _____DAY OF _____, _____

READ A SECOND TIME THIS _____ DAY OF _____, ____

READ A THIRD TIME THIS _____ DAY OF _____, _____

RECONSIDERED, PASSED AND FINALLY ADOPTED THIS
_____ DAY OF _____, _____

returning to the work site, the Inspector found that the work had proceeded without any alteration and that the garage was a two-storey structure. The Contractor said the second storey was for a studio, but the Inspector noted that the roughed in plumbing indicated the space could be used as a suite. The Inspector again issued a stop-work order, but the Contractor kept on building. The Building Inspector, in consultation with the City Administrator and legal counsel, began legal proceedings to get the situation corrected. They did not apply for an injunction to stop the work because, by the time they had the paper work in order, the exterior of the building was finished. Instead, they gave notice to the Building Contractor that the work did not comply with the city's by-laws and had to be removed.

The Contractor immediately sought the assistance of his friend the Real Estate Agent, who advised him to seek mercy from council. The Building Contractor had spent $55,000 on the extension of the house, and $28,000 on the construction of the studio/garage, not to mention $31,000 on the renovation of the kitchen and the existing garage. All of the money had been borrowed on his line of credit at the bank.

The next-door neighbour has realized that the new studio/garage will mean that her patio will be in perpetual shade because the building exceeds the legally permitted height. She has hired the Solicitor to make sure that the city protects her interests. The Real Estate Agent arranged with the City Administrator to have the Administrator submit a report to council outlining the facts of the matter, and to allow the Real Estate Agent and the Building Contractor to appear at the council meeting to discuss the matter with the city council. The Solicitor learned of this arrangement and will also be present at the meeting.

10.16 Fees for Public Skating

The City Treasurer recommended an increase in the fees for public skating. In the course of the budget discussions, council had approved a 4 per cent increase and included the additional revenue in the budget. City council, however, did not specify how the increase should be implemented. The Treasurer made it an "across the board" increase, and the fees were rounded off to make it easier for the cashier to make change. A variety of people have lobbied members of council, insisting that it is unfair to apply the rate increase for children, "Moms and Kids" programs, and senior citizens. The increase, they say, should apply to adults only (and few adults pay for public skating).

The by-law to give effect to the increases has been presented to council for its first three readings. A copy of the by-law can be found in Figure 10.13. Table 10.11 shows the estimated revenues by type (with and without the fee increase).

If a council member does not agree with the fee structure proposed in the by-law, he or she will have to move an amendment.

10.17 Massage Therapy Issue

Two women moved into the bungalow behind the high school about four months ago. They have been quite quiet, and there has been little traffic in or out of their house. Neighbours have noticed that they are "night owls" because the lights in the house seem to be on virtually all night, but no one has complained about them. About the same time that they moved into their house, notices began to appear about "massage therapists" who were available 24 hours a day for "personal services." No one made the connection until the police asked the Building Inspector to intervene because, police alleged, the women were operating a home-based business out of a residential

TABLE 10.11 Public Skating Revenues by Source

Category	Annual Revenue —Existing Rates	Annual Revenue —Revised Rates	Existing Admission Fee	Revised Admission Fee
Adult Skating	$600	$626	$3.50	$3.65
Senior Citizens Skating	$200	$210	$2.00	$2.10
Moms & Kids Skating	$3,200	$3,360	$2.00	$2.10
Teens (13–19)	$7,000	$7,350	$3.00	$3.15
Children (12 & under)	$8,500	$8,925	$1.00	$1.05
Total	**$19,500**	**$20,471**		

property. More to the point, the police advised the Building Inspector that it was a call-girl business, and that massage therapy was merely a front. The Building Inspector, of course, investigated and found that, indeed, the women were operating an escort and massage therapy business from their home. However, no customers came to their house, and the women did not meet with any customers themselves. They merely recruited individuals whom they would dispatch (by telephone) to meet with customers in another location. The Building Inspector found that they had applied for, and received, a business licence for a massage therapy business. The Inspector also found that the business licence by-law is rather poorly written and that no detailed definition of "massage therapy" was included in the by-law.

While investigating, the Building Inspector had discussed the issue with the women's neighbours, and the rumours immediately began to circulate. By the time Councillor #3 heard about it, the rumour was that a full-fledged brothel was operating next to the high school, which of course was not the case. By this time, the school principal had given an interview to the radio station emphasizing how badly this situation would influence the school's students, and a member of the police force had told the radio station that the business was simply a front for prostitution and was run by "organized crime."

Councillor #3 gave "notice of motion" that the business licence should be revoked. This motion is to be the subject of debate at the council meeting. The women have hired the Solicitor to represent them. They want the matter adjourned until they can present a full defence. They believe that they are doing nothing illegal. (In fact, the police force has laid no charges against them, their employees, or their clients.)

10.18 Are Five Cars Too Many?

A complaint has been received by Councillor #4 about a property on Ridgeview Drive. The owner of the property has five cars in the front yard. All are more or less complete, but none can be driven. The owner (Ridgeview Drive Resident) insists that the cars (all of which are from model years 1962 through 1967) are collector cars and are to be restored to their former glory. The neighbours claim that the cars are "junk." The zoning by-law

FIGURE 10.14

The Summerville Sentinel

EDITORIAL

Big Box Retail Development — Clearly the Way to Go

MUCH HAS BEEN SAID in recent years about the impact that globalization is having on our way of life. At the community level, globalization, in the form of large multinational retail corporations, is changing the face of our cities and towns. Critics argue that these corporations, with their big retail outlets on the edge of town, "suck" the life out of the traditional place of business in most communities—the downtown core. Proponents, however, say that such developments have a positive impact on communities by providing jobs, more choice, and lower prices. In their opinion, globalization is something that cannot and should not be resisted.

The recent proposal to create a big box retail development in Summerville means that globalization is knocking on the door of our fair city. There are some who say we should keep the door firmly shut—our downtown core needs to be protected from the marauding onslaught of the global economy. Although valiantly defiant in the face of change, this approach is problematic: one small city cannot fight the new world order. Globalization will change our downtown core whether we open the door or not. And maybe that's not such a bad thing. Maybe it's time that our downtown finds its own niche in the global economy, just as other downtowns in other parts of the country have done in recent years. Someone once said that if you ignore the past, you are doomed to repeat it. You might also say that if you ignore the future, you are doomed to suffer the consequences. Yes, this city needs a revitalized downtown. But it also needs jobs and the type of economic activity that could come from a big box retail development. Who knows, maybe the proposed development will be just the tonic we need to realize both of these goals.

for the rural area states that you cannot store more than two cars on a property, unless a building or a fence encloses them.

Councillor #4 has asked that the item be placed on the council agenda. No notice of motion was given, and it is not known if Councillor #4 is simply seeking information or may perhaps want to give direction to city staff. The Ridgeview Drive Resident knows that council will be discussing the cars and plans to be in the audience for the council meeting.

10.19 Skateboard Problems

Many of the young people in Summerville have taken to using their skateboards to travel from the secondary school through the centre of town to the most popular teen hangout, located a few doors to the south of Riverside Anglican Church. They are not always as careful as they might be, and there have been a few "near misses" as the skateboarders (almost all young boys) have "whizzed by" some of the town's elderly residents.

Councillor #4 has been approached by several of these residents, who want council to put a stop to this practice. Councillor #4 has asked that the item be placed on the agenda, and will plead for the rest of council to find a way to stop the use of skateboards in the downtown. One idea is the creation of a skateboard park. The costs of this project, however, are unknown and would have to be covered by the city if private funders cannot be found.

10.20 "Big Box" Retail

A major real estate developer (the "Big Box" Developer) from Douglas has applied for rezoning of a parcel of land on the east bench, to the east of the OSB Plant. The intention is to develop a "big box" retail development. It would have three buildings of 12,000 square metres each. The names of the prospective tenants are a closely guarded secret, but speculation has it that the tenants include a home renovation centre, a large hardware chain, and a discount supermarket. There is also provision for two fast-food outlets and one gas station on the site. The site is adjacent to the existing highway and, therefore, to the rumoured relocation of the provincial highway (see the site plan in Figure 10.15). It is projected that the development will create 30 full-time jobs and 90 part-time jobs, once it is fully operational. The proposal has been the topic of discussion for some time, with residents of the community picking sides. Some fear that it will be the end of the downtown, and others see it as a great opportunity to bring Summerville into the twenty-first century.

The city council is to hold a public hearing on the proposal. Everyone knows the issues, and it has been agreed that the speakers' list will be limited to the "Big Box" Developer, the Real Estate Agent, the Wild Flower Lady, the Solicitor (appearing on behalf of downtown property owners), the Casino Developer, and the owner of the pub and motel.

The fact that the proposal has proceeded to the public hearing stage means that the city council has given the rezoning by-law its first two readings. If the council gives the by-law a third reading after the hearing, the by-law can be adopted at the next council meeting, and the "Big Box" Developer will be able to go ahead with the project.

10.21 Speeding Taxi Driver

Provincial legislation provides that applicants for taxi driver licences can appeal to the municipal council in the event that the police chief denies their application for a licence. The police chief has refused to renew the taxi driver licence for Speedy Taxi Driver on the grounds that the driver has had three speeding tickets in the past two years. Two of the tickets were for speeding in the school zone adjacent to the secondary school. In their report on the matter, police officers observed that the Speedy Taxi Driver had come to their attention during various alcohol-related investigations but that no charges or convictions resulted from the investigations.

Council will hold a hearing on the issue, at which time the taxi driver will be given the opportunity to present reasons why the licence to operate a taxi should be renewed.

10.22 Non-Resident Use of City Recreation Facilities

Councillor #1 is very concerned about the budget difficulties facing the city and has concluded that at least some of the budget pressures could be reduced if residents of Steamboat Bend and Valley

View shouldered some of the costs of parks, recreation, police protection, and other city services. After all, the councillor reasons, residents of these two areas come into the city to use all of these services. In light of the city's inability to persuade the property owners in these areas to accept extension of the city boundary, Councillor #1 thinks that the solution is to make non-residents pay more for the use of city services. Therefore, Councillor #1 intends to give the following notice of motion: "That city administration be instructed to draft amendments to all the by-laws authorizing fees and charges so that non-resident fees will be twice the amount charged to city residents for the use of any city service or facility."

This motion would be considered at the council meeting following the meeting at which it is introduced.

10.23 Renewal of Downtown Sidewalks

The downtown sidewalks are quite old and present a tripping hazard. News of the possible Centrum Hotel and Casino has led many of the property owners to think of renewal and expansion of their buildings to cater to the many new customers that the hotel and casino will bring. Over the regular morning coffee at the Summerville Hotel, the Hardware Store Owner convinced fellow coffee-drinkers that the city should be asked to install new, decorative sidewalks throughout the downtown, along with new street lights, sign posts, and street trees, on the grounds that this would be something that would benefit the city as a whole, and should be paid for by the city. Everyone agreed, and the Hardware Store Owner was "elected" to get a delegation together and go to a council meeting to make the proposal. Arrangements have been made with the City Clerk for this issue to be on the agenda for Council Meeting #5.

The Pub and Motel Owner was tipped off by Councillor #2 and will be in the gallery at the council meeting. While in favour of making the downtown look better, the Pub and Motel Owner does not think that property taxes on the pub and motel should be used to benefit downtown property owners, and will attempt to present that point of view to council.

10.24 Accessing Pornography at the Library

The President of the Fire Fighters' Union has found out that pornography is being accessed on the library's computer. His wife happened to be passing by the library's public access computers (made available so that library users can have free access to the Internet) and noticed that a teen was viewing inappropriate pictures. She confronted the Librarian, only to be told that there was nothing that could be done to prevent people from using the computers for that purpose. The Librarian did, however, agree to speak to the youth in question and to reposition the computer screen so that people passing by the computer workstation could not view it.

This was a hot topic of conversation at the dinner table, and it led to the President of the Fire Fighters' Union making a complaint to the Acting Mayor. The gist of the complaint was that the library should be monitoring the use of the computers, including identifying what web pages people were accessing, and that the library should deny computer use to people who access pornography or other inappropriate sites. Although he gave no definition of pornography, he would probably have defined much late night television programming as such.

The Acting Mayor agreed that council should discuss the matter because the city provides most of the library's money. The Librarian has been invited to attend the council meeting to tell council what the library will do to prevent people from looking at pornography sites.

10.25 Purchase or Lease?

Councillor #3 is concerned that not enough money is being spent on road rehabilitation and the replacement of equipment for the public works department. The councillor believes that the condition of the roads could be vastly improved within a year or two if the city would simply borrow the money and undertake a major paving program. As the councillor says, "That is what a business would do." In other words, a business that let its business premises fall into disrepair would not do a bit of refurbishing at a time. It would do it all at once, to minimize delay and inconvenience and to get a "better bang for the buck." Councillor #3

FIGURE 10.15

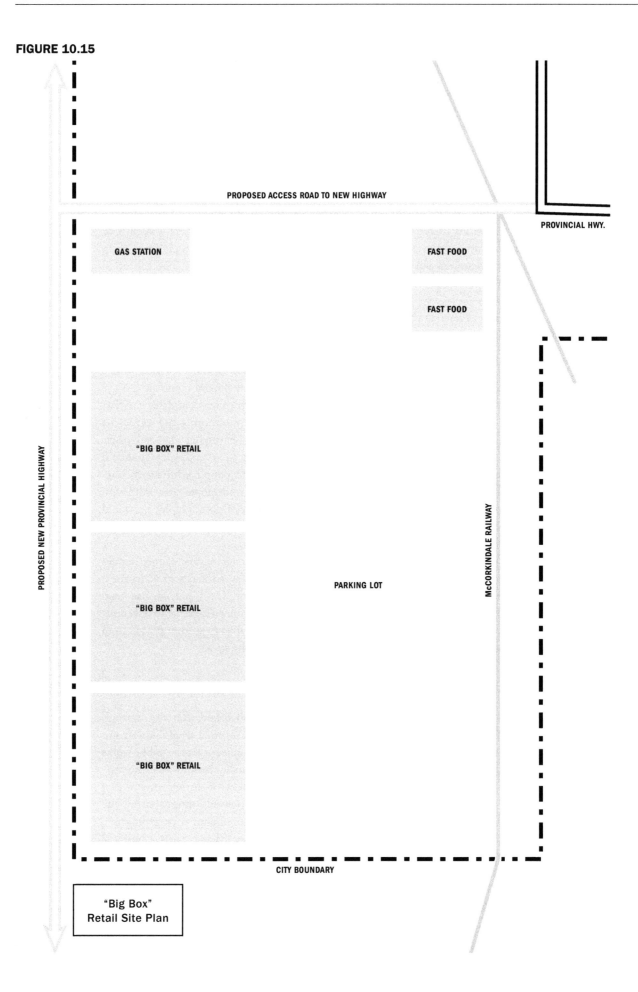

PROPOSED ACCESS ROAD TO NEW HIGHWAY

PROVINCIAL HWY.

GAS STATION

FAST FOOD

FAST FOOD

PROPOSED NEW PROVINCIAL HIGHWAY

McCORKINDALE RAILWAY

"BIG BOX" RETAIL

"BIG BOX" RETAIL

PARKING LOT

"BIG BOX" RETAIL

CITY BOUNDARY

"Big Box"
Retail Site Plan

is also of the view that it does not make sense to purchase equipment. Equipment, according to business practice, should be leased. Councillor #3 was opposed to the creation of the reserve for equipment replacement last year.

With these thoughts in mind, Councillor #3 proposed a motion at a previous council meeting to

» Spend the equipment replacement reserve on paving,

» Establish a city policy that all equipment be leased, and

» Borrow $4.5 million to undertake a major paving program.

The motion was tabled by council to be discussed after the completion of the current year's budget. It was council's view that Councillor #3's ideas were worth debating but that the pressure of current events did not allow for a full discussion of the issues. The City Clerk will place the issue on an agenda for the council meeting immediately after the current year's budget is adopted.

10.26 Imposing Development Cost Charges

The City Administrator has watched with growing alarm the development proposals for the community. If the experience of other communities is a guide, the casino and the "big box" retail developments are likely to create a need for significant improvements in utilities and roads. It is possible that the city might be required to share in the cost of some kind of highway interchange to serve the proposed "big box" stores, and, based on some preliminary data, it is probable that the city will have to upgrade the sanitary and storm sewers to handle the casino (if it is built).

The Administrator has decided to ask the council for authority to begin studying how and when development cost charges (impost fees) might be imposed so that developers would pay for expenditures such as those cited above. There has been some disagreement among the administration's staff. The Treasurer has been forthright, expressing the view that Summerville desperately needs new investment and that development cost charges will be a disincentive to development.

This item will be placed on the agenda after the adoption of the annual budget, at a time of the Administrator's choosing.

10.27 "It Was, And Is, A Good Deal."

A member of the community has advised the Acting Mayor that the public works department has used improper procedures to purchase a large amount of park supplies. Minor purchase orders are supposed to be used to authorize expenditures of less than $400. When expenditures are more than $400, a variety of competitive bidding processes must be used. For example, two telephone quotations are to be obtained if the purchase is expected to be less than $4,000, three written quotations are to be obtained if the purchase is expected to cost between $4,000 and $10,000, and formal public tenders or requests for proposals must be used when expenditures are more than $10,000. It seems that five minor purchase orders were issued to authorize a single shipment of lawn fertilizer, and the purchase of a motorized mower for the parks was broken into three components (garden tractor, mower deck, and cutting bag) so that telephone quotations could be sought for each component.

The Acting Mayor made enquiries through the City Administrator and others and feels that there are grounds to believe that the required procedures are not being followed. On the surface, it would appear that certain local suppliers (as yet unnamed) are being favoured, while others are excluded from city business. On the other hand, staff members indicate that following the procedures requires a great deal of staff time, the cost of which likely exceeds any savings that might be obtained from competitive bidding. In the case of the mower, they point out that they knew that the supplier of the lawn mower was prepared to give a very good price on a unit that was on hand and that the city saved a lot of money by buying that unit. The staff also claim that the supplier of the fertilizer had too much in inventory, and also sold it to the city at a very low price—a better price than would have been obtained had written quotations been sought.

FIGURE 10.16

Cascadian Times

Feds to Sell Former Army Base

By Harriet Swackhammer

In a widely anticipated move following its surprise election victory 3 months ago, the federal government today announced its intention to sell off large amounts of federal property around the country. The policy of privatizing federal property was a key part of the Conservative Party's platform in the recent election, so it is no surprise that the government has followed through with this promise. Properties affected include army bases, ports, parks, and buildings in urban areas. In Cascadia, the main affected property is the former army base in Summerville. The base was closed in 1995, and the property has remained vacant and largely unused since then. Over the years, several developers have offered to purchase the property, pro-

posing projects ranging from an amusement park and a shopping complex to a housing development. The previous federal government, however, refused to sell. The present government's change of direction on this matter opens the door for development and for the possible involvement of the municipal government in this process. In a speech to the Local Government Association of Cascadia (LGAC) in Douglas yesterday, federal Minister for Public Works Jim Kinsley indicated that the fate of federal property around the country could be connected to the government's much-heralded "New Deal" for municipalities.

The Acting Mayor has asked that the matter be placed on council's agenda in order to make council aware of the situation and seek guidance as to how to proceed to deal with the allegations.

10.28 Economic Development Commission

Members of the Summerville Chamber of Commerce executive have not been satisfied with council's efforts to promote economic development in the community. They recognize that the city has expended a reasonable amount of money to advertise the community. But they believe that the city falls short in providing data to prospective businesses and in recruiting new businesses. This has been a long-standing issue with the chamber.

Some members of city council, however, feel that the problem is really with the chamber. The city provides an annual grant to the chamber ($35,000), which they believe is more than suf-

ficient. Councillors feel that the chamber has not spent that money effectively.

The Chair of the Chamber of Commerce and the executive have contacted a number of other communities and have determined that most of them have a city-financed organization that is devoted to economic development, often in association with the local chamber of commerce. They have arranged to appear before council with a request that the city establish an Economic Development Commission.

10.29 Surplus Federal Lands

The Acting Mayor has received a letter from Public Works Canada indicating that the former army base, which was closed several years ago, is surplus to its needs and, as such, the federal government wishes to sell the property. Since the federal government has left little time for a response, the Acting Mayor has invited the Real

Estate Developer, the Chair of the Chamber of Commerce, and the Planner to meet with council to discuss how the city should respond to the letter.

10.30 "It's Ours To Spend."

Summerville's "Founders Day" will be celebrated in one week. Four members of council decided, in a late night session after a council meeting three weeks ago, that it would be a great idea to have the city sponsor a "splashy" and "impressive" float in the parade and a teen dance in the evening. They arranged with the Hardware Store Owner to purchase paint, ribbons, and a variety of hardware necessary to decorate the city's flatbed truck, and they hired a local band (for $2,500) to play at the teen dance. They also agreed to pay the Summerville Boosters Club $1,200 to operate a concession stand during the dance, and to pay the Door Maker $800 to help construct the float. As an afterthought, they arranged to have the fire department participate in the parade, even though that will mean calling four fire fighters in on overtime in order to provide the minimum number of fire fighters needed to staff the fire halls.

Councillor #2 was not at the meeting and heard about the arrangements from the Fire Fighters' Union President, who is one of the fire fighters called in to work overtime. Councillor #2 checked with the City Administrator and found that there is no provision in the budget for the expenditures and that no purchase orders have been issued by city staff for the materials. The manager for the dance band has confirmed the arrangements, as has the Door Maker.

Councillor #2 will rise on a point of order at the council meeting, requesting information and assurance that the city is not committed or obligated to this expenditure of money. The City Administrator will advise council that, unless council approves payment, these invoices will remain unpaid.

10.31 Commuter Suburb

A developer from Youngston is interested in buying a large portion of the closed army base to build a housing development. The proposed development would be located 10 km to the north of Summerville and about 120 km south of Jackson and Manchester, communities that are suburbs of Youngston. The developer thinks that this development, comprised of single-family homes and located on a very scenic stretch of the Spring River, would appeal to people working in Jackson and Manchester. The commute would take approximately 1.25 hours (in good weather). The developer, however, may face opposition from some residents of Summerville, who want to make this area into a nature preserve, and from the provincial police force, which is looking to locate its main training centre on the site of the old army base. There is also the issue of who is responsible for cleaning up leftover ordnance from when the base was used as a firing range.

The developer has asked the City Administrator to write a letter of support for the proposal. The Administrator has, in turn, arranged for the matter to be placed on the council agenda, so councillors can signal whether or not they are in agreement with the proposal. This issue has been well publicized and is well known to those in the community who support alternative uses of the land.

10.32 Retirement Resort

A developer from Douglas wants to build a luxury retirement resort on the site of the old sewer plant in the southern part of Summerville, just inside the city boundaries. The resort would be located on a scenic part of the Spring River (although one that has been prone to flooding in the past), near to the local hospital and the proposed "big box" retail development. The development could provide a significant boost to the local economy in the long term. The site, however, has recently been tested, and it is contaminated with toxic chemicals. If the development is going to go ahead, the city will be responsible for cleaning up the site, as well as shoring up the riverbank to ensure that the effects of flooding are minimized. Together, these projects could cost upwards of $1 million.

The developer has asked council to authorize the expenditures and to sell the land to the developer at a price that would cover the anticipated remediation costs. Council must decide how to respond to the developer's request.

ELEVEN

Characters

In the following pages, you will find information on the characters that are featured in this simulation, together with some comments on how to play these roles. The characters are presented in alphabetical order. There may be more characters than there are participants in the simulation. In that case, some participants will have to play more than one role. Your instructor will advise you about the roles you are playing.

A brief character sketch is provided for each of the characters in the simulation. We have developed these to provide you with some "clues" as to how each of the roles should be played and to ensure that a wide range of views are brought out in the course of the simulation. You should remember that, in playing your role, you are not playing yourself. You are playing a character. Now is your chance to practise for the Oscar, or the Gemini, and to hone your acting skills. Try to make your character realistic. Anticipate what your character would do in certain circumstances, especially when interacting with the other characters in

the simulation. What points would the character make? What biases would she or he bring to the discussions? How would the character's values differ from those of other characters? Do not feel the need to be continually witty, charming, glib, or erudite. Most people, in real life, don't behave this way. They stutter, pause, think, start a sentence and change their minds and start again. So, do not be disappointed if you do this too.

The information on the characters is also intended to provide you with an indication of what you might expect from the characters with whom you will be interacting. You can use that information to form a preliminary opinion about how they might be expected to react to various situations or issues.

In addition, your instructor has supplemental information for you (and only for you) to help you play your specific role. That information may include hints or suggestions about what issues to become involved in and how you might be involved.

11.1 Auto Wrecker

The Auto Wrecker runs a garage and auto wrecking business in Steamboat Bend. His property is located adjacent to the highway and consists of a three-bay garage, a large storage area, and his residence. He has lived in Steamboat Bend for many years and has been a fierce opponent of joining the City of Summerville. He is concerned that city regulations may make it difficult for him to continue his business, and he does not see why he should pay for city services that he does not use (such as the swimming pool and library). In addition, he believes that higher taxes would make his business uneconomical.

The recent fire has caused him to have a slight change in position. As a devoted family man, he now realizes how much danger his family faces because of the lack of fire protection. He feels that the city should provide fire protection to Steamboat Bend as a gesture of goodwill, since it would not increase the city's operating costs in any way. Fires are relatively rare, and he can remember only two small fires since he moved to Steamboat Bend (not counting the latest house fire).

11.2
Beautician

The Beautician is a widow with a five-year-old son and three-year-old daughter. After her husband died, she renewed her beautician's licence and opened a beauty salon in her basement recreation room, but she had to close it down because it was not permitted under current zoning regulations.

She moved to Summerville when she got married, having lived previously in a small community about 30 kilometres away. She leads a relatively quiet life. She is on good terms with her neighbours, but none is a close friend. Her children keep her very busy, and she does not participate in any church or social groups.

11.3 "Big Box" Developer

The "Big Box" Developer lives in Douglas, the provincial capital. The Developer has an outstanding track record, involving some of the best residential and commercial developments in the province. A recent mixed-use residential, office and retail development in Douglas won many international awards for design, environmental excellence, and marketing. The Developer has found ways to make low-income housing work in urban developments and is well regarded within the non-market housing community for innovative solutions.

The Developer heard about the relocation of the highway over cocktails (the relocation plans are not a well-kept secret), and was able to get an option on the property in Summerville. The commercial attractions were obvious, and there was not much difficulty in signing up potential tenants. The Developer has refused to identify the potential tenants in any way. No one knows if the food chain that operates the grocery store on Valley Drive is one of the tenants.

The Developer is not particularly concerned about the hotel and casino project, as it will not impact in any way on the "big box" retail development. It is the highway relocation that is the major concern. If the highway is not relocated, the "big box" development would not be as profitable, as people from other towns would be less likely to visit the "big box" stores if they had to follow the existing convoluted highway route. Political contacts have assured the Developer that there is no chance that the highway relocation would be "shelved" if the hotel and casino project were approved, and the Developer has made those assurances well known within the community.

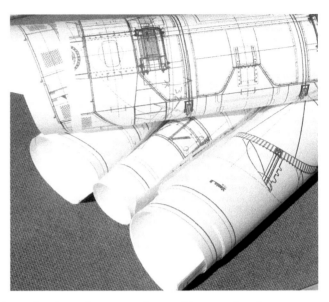

11.4 Building Contractor

The Building Contractor has been in business for about five years, after working as a framing carpenter for other contractors in Summerville. The Building Contractor is considered a good worker, but is also known to be willing to "skirt around" the rules from time to time. The city building inspectors have learned that they need to watch the Building Contractor's work closely, but, every time that they have identified an issue that required that work be redone, the Building Contractor has willingly complied.

The Building Contractor is not particularly wealthy and, in recent years, building activity has been rather slow. This means that the Contractor has had time to work on the family house, which is mortgaged to the limit. The Building Contractor's line of credit is also exhausted. He rushed to complete the exterior of his house before winter and still has to complete much of the interior finishing.

11.5 Building Inspector

The Building Inspector is responsible for issuing building permits and inspecting building construction to ensure that it complies with the building code and the zoning by-law. In Summerville, the Building Inspector also serves as the Business Licence Inspector. Summerville's Building Inspector is a former carpenter who has been an inspector for four years and is very knowledgeable about building codes and construction but not about law enforcement, the rights of the city to enforce compliance, or the drafting or interpretation of by-laws.

11.6 Casino Developer

The Casino Developer's father is the founder of the casino company. A recent graduate of the business administration program at the University of Cascadia, the Casino Developer has been made responsible for the identification of new business opportunities and for strategic planning. The Developer's role is largely to achieve the goals set by the founder, which, in this case, is to get quick approval of what both think will be a very profitable enterprise. The Casino Developer lives in Douglas and has been sent to Summerville to assist the Real Estate Developer in negotiations with the city.

11.7
Chair, Chamber of Commerce

The Chair of the Chamber of Commerce is a young executive with a local insurance company. A native of Summerville who studied business administration at the University of Churchill, and who is known to be something of a "go-getter" and a "builder," the Chair has an intense desire to see Summerville become a more important community. The Chair's view (which is shared by some members of the chamber executive) is that Summerville lacks the appropriate organizations to promote economic development.

11.8 Chair of the Recreation Commission

The Chair of the Recreation Commission has been active in youth sports organizations for some time. A parent of three boys, the Chair served on the executive of the minor hockey association and the lacrosse association. The Chair operates a small construction company that specializes in excavations, gravel hauling, and road grading and has aspirations of running for a seat on city council.

11.9 City Administrator

The City Administrator has lived in Summerville for just over 10 years. The Administrator is 54 years old and has two years to go until retirement. With over 30 years of experience in local government (having worked in a variety of small and medium-size municipalities with distinction), the Administrator is a stickler for following the local government legislation, and making sure that all the "i's are dotted and the t's are crossed." The Administrator is a good delegator and works well with council.

The City Administrator and partner (who is a teacher) live in Royal Heights. They have no children.

The City Administrator is charged with the overall management of the operations of the city; ensuring that policies, programs, and directions of council are implemented; and advising and informing the council on the operation and affairs of the city.

11.10
City Clerk

The City Clerk has lived in Summerville for close to 20 years. Although starting with the city as an office clerk without much postsecondary education, the City Clerk has managed to climb the career ladder over time and was hired into the clerk's position about five years ago. The Clerk has taken some university courses and, consequently, has received an Intermediate Certificate in Local Government Administration. Very proud of these accomplishments, of the work undertaken by the clerk's office, and of the services that the city provides, the City Clerk has no aspirations to become the City Administrator or to move to a position in a larger community.

The City Clerk is married, and the couple lives with one of their two children (the other is at university) in the McGregor subdivision.

In addition to the duties enumerated below, the City Clerk has been appointed as the chief electoral officer for Summerville. The City Clerk is responsible for ensuring that accurate minutes of the council meetings and committees are prepared and that the minutes, by-laws, and other records of the business of council and its committees are maintained and kept safe. The Clerk is also responsible for ensuring that access is provided to the records as required by law or authorized by council, for administering oaths, certifying copies of by-laws, and accepting notices or other documents that are served on the city. The Clerk conducts correspondence for the council, arranges the council agendas, and is responsible for managing the city's activities under access to information and protection of privacy legislation.

11.11
City Planner

A graduate of the School of Planning at King's University in Douglas, the City Planner has worked in four different municipalities in various junior planning positions. The Planner has now begun a career as an independent consultant to a number of municipalities like Summerville. The Planner believes that development must be carefully controlled to protect both the environment and the interests of city residents and to promote efficient economic development in the community. The Planner is opposed to urban sprawl, and is a strong advocate of the "new urbanism."

Married with one small daughter (aged three), the Planner lives in a rented house in the North Bench subdivision.

11.12 City Treasurer

The City Treasurer is approaching 45 years of age and took the position of treasurer because it seemed like a good way to gain the experience necessary to move into a similar position in a much bigger community. The Treasurer is a qualified chartered accountant and has worked in two other municipalities (as an accountant in one municipality and as a deputy treasurer in another, both of which were about Summerville's size). The Treasurer has worked in Summerville for almost two years and is now beginning to respond to notices of vacancies at other municipalities.

The Treasurer is regarded as a competent accountant but a rather conservative and cautious individual. The Treasurer is married and lives with a spouse and two teenaged sons in a modest house in Vista View subdivision.

The City Treasurer is responsible for receiving all money paid to the city, ensuring the keeping of all funds and securities held by the city, investing municipal funds, paying bills on behalf of the city, ensuring that accurate and full financial records are kept, and exercising control and supervision over all other financial affairs of the city. In addition, the Treasurer plays a lead role in the preparation of the budget. The Treasurer supervises an accounting staff, including cashiers, accounting clerks, accounts payable clerks, and tax and utility clerks. The Treasurer also acts as the city's purchasing agent.

11.13 Councillor #1

Councillor #1 is 52 years old. He is married and has three daughters, the eldest of which is in grade 12 and is a member of the Senior Girls Volleyball Team. The other daughters are in grades 7 and 9. Councillor #1 and family have lived in Summerville for 29 years, having moved to Summerville all those years ago so he could article with a local firm of chartered accountants. He is currently one of three partners in this firm, which has ten other employees. The majority of their clients are small businesses such as retail stores, independent loggers, trucking contractors, and mechanics. The firm does a few audits. The partnership prospered until the 1980s, when business began to decline along with the decline in the overall level of economic activity in the city. The loss of the head offices of the sawmill companies had a significant impact on the firm's billings. One of the firm's partners will be retiring in the next three or four years. Until then, Councillor #1's income will be constrained because the firm does not really generate enough income to support three partners. Councillor #1 has considered seeking the office of mayor, but has some concerns about the timing. He and his wife seem to have reached an agreement that it would be best if he delayed running for mayor until their youngest child is in high school.

Councillor #1 married shortly after articling. The councillor's spouse, who came to Summerville to work at the local hospital, is currently 44 and is employed by the Summerville Regional Health Board as a public health nurse. They live in a modest house on about 0.5 ha of land in South Bench. Councillor #1 is an avid hunter and something of a carpenter, and he is active in Ducks Unlimited and the Summerville Rod and Gun Club. His wife is an ardent gardener, particularly noted for her ability to grow tomatoes and corn. She has become quite concerned about pollution and air quality issues in recent years, and she now attends most community meetings that deal with environmental issues. She does not, however, play a leadership role at these meetings. Previously an avid member of the school's parent advisory council, she gave up this interest in order to make time available to drive the Senior Girls Volleyball Team to games (most of which are out of town).

11.14 Councillor #2

Councillor #2 was just recently elected to council. Councillor #2 has lived in the community for seven years and is a vice-principal of one of the elementary schools. Prior to moving to Summerville, Councillor #2 had been a teacher in a slightly larger neighbouring city and a member of that community's Library Board, Advisory Planning Commission, and Recreation Commission. Councillor #2 married shortly after moving to Summerville. The couple lives in the old part of downtown. (They lived next door to the Fire Fighters' Union President until he moved to Royal Heights.) The two couples are friendly, having met through their church.

Councillor #2 decided to seek elected office in order to do something about the lack of wholesome youth activities in Summerville. Councillor #2 has no aspirations for higher office.

11.15 Councillor #3

Councillor #3 is nearing completion of a third term of office. Councillor #3 is separated and lives alone in the once-shared family home in the River's Edge subdivision. The Councillor's four children have all left home and are pursuing careers in other parts of the country. Councillor #3 has operated a successful parts supply business for over 20 years. It is located on Valley Drive in the light industrial area.

A strong supporter of the concept of free enterprise, Councillor #3 is sceptical of many aspects of government regulation, feeling that regulations dampen enterprise and economic growth. Nonetheless, Councillor #3 does recognize that the city has to impose some order on the way in which growth occurs, simply to control its own costs. Generally speaking, Councillor #3 does not support the concept of "big government." However, Councillor #3 is a strong supporter of "family values" and believes that government has a role to play in reinforcing those values.

The vast majority of Councillor #3's time is devoted to council business and the operation of the parts supply business, but the councillor does find time to participate in the noon-hour business service club meetings once a week and in the Summerville Chamber of Commerce (where Councillor #3 is currently on the board of directors). Councillor #3 is the city's representative on the board of the regional government. It was Councillor #3 who suggested to the regional board that it might ask the city to provide fire protection to Steamboat Bend. Councillor #3 has some aspirations to run either in the next provincial election or the next federal election (depending on whether the current incumbents run again), and the councillor wonders whether service as mayor would be an advantage in seeking higher office.

11.16 Councillor #4

Councillor #4 is 68 years old and has lived in Summerville for almost 40 years. At one time or another, Councillor #4 has been active in almost every community organization, having served on the boards of the Minor Hockey Association, the local theatrical society, Little League, the Fall Fair Society, the Scouts Canada District Council, the Music Festival Society, and the Summerville Horticultural Club. Although Councillor #4 is no longer on any of these boards, seven terms on council have given Councillor #4 ample opportunity to maintain a wide network of contacts. Indeed, people say that few citizens of Summerville have as many contacts in such diverse parts of the community.

Councillor #4 and partner live in a small house near the central business district that they have occupied for many years. While they live on a fixed income (being retirees from the provincial civil service), they have a relatively comfortable life, particularly since most of their leisure activities consist of attending a myriad of civic events. Councillor #4 can always be counted on to be available to bring greetings from council to conferences, wedding anniversaries, graduation dinners, and year-end league dinners.

Councillor #4 has no known political affiliations or aspirations. In fact, Councillor #4 seldom expresses any views on political issues. Councillor #4 focuses almost exclusively on trying to help people get things done by giving them advice, opening doors, and giving moral support to "good causes."

11.17 Councillor #5

Councillor #5 is one of Summerville's "new generation" of local politicians. A recent graduate of the Environmental Planning and Forestry Program at Youngston University, Councillor #5 is employed by the provincial government's forest service, with responsibility for monitoring the forest industry's compliance with various codes and regulations regarding logging and road construction. Councillor #5 has little regard for "old time" politicians, and is intent on pursuing higher office. Councillor #5 was elected on a "green" platform, largely related to preserving the river valley and keeping Summerville a pleasant "small town" where people can walk to work and recreation.

Councillor #5 is unmarried, with no known romantic relationships in Summerville. Councillor #5 lives in a small house north of the high school.

11.18 Councillor #6

Councillor #6 has served two terms on the Summerville City Council. A sawmill employee, Councillor #6 served on the mill's safety committee, on the committee that managed the mill's employee assistance plan, and on the union executive. Councillor #6 loves fishing and is an avid student of local history.

Councillor #6 lives in South Bench and is married. Councillor #6 has two teenaged children (one boy and one girl), and both have had some behavioural problems. In fact, the daughter has been barred from public skating at the arena because of a vandalism incident.

11.19
Door Maker

The Door Maker owns and operates Summerville Sash and Door, which is located in the light industrial area just south of the highway and adjacent to the river. The plant is relatively small and, in the face of competition from "big box" building supply firms in neighbouring cities, is having a hard time remaining in business. There is nothing wrong with the quality of the product. It is simply a question of scale. This small business cannot attain the economies of scale that its major competitors can. The Door Maker has just one full-time employee. However, he has a network of part-time workers that he can call on if he requires extra labour.

11.20 Elementary School Teacher

The Elementary School Teacher is responsible for the computer resources in all the elementary schools in town. The Teacher learned about the pornography at the library issue at a Sunday church service (in the course of a discussion with the wife of the President of the Fire Fighters' Union). In dealing with children's use of computers, the Teacher has found that it is essential to have programs that limit the type of websites that can be accessed, as well as to keep records of what people do on the computers. The Teacher intends to be in the gallery when the Librarian is heard, and to make sure that council either requires the library to impose better controls or get rid of the public computer terminals. After all, the Teacher thinks that the schools already have computers with Internet access so children do not need to access them at the library and that adults should pay for their own computers.

11.21 Hardware Store Owner

Summerville is blessed with an old-fashioned hardware store, filled with odd fittings, tools, and parts as well as a wide range of household appliances, kitchen utensils, and more. It is a throwback to the 1940s. The Hardware Store Owner is the third generation operator and a prominent member of the Riverside Anglican Church congregation.

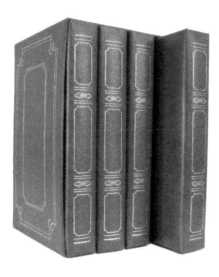

11.22
Librarian

The Librarian is a recent graduate from the University of Cascadia, with a master's degree in library science, and was appointed to the position of librarian very recently. A single person, the Librarian seems to "escape" to Youngston or Douglas on days off, and is not well known in the community.

11.23
Massage
Therapist

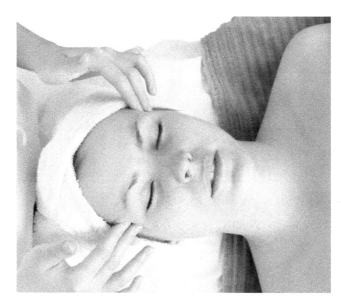

The Massage Therapist moved to Summerville about six months ago with her partner and purchased a small house. She is middle aged, and has carried on her business so as to avoid attracting attention. She and her partner were drawn to Summerville because they identified it as a town in which there was little or no competition for the services they wanted to provide. They believed that there was a market for their services, which consisted of arranging for very discreet "companions" to meet with customers (some of whom actually wanted and received a massage). From their experience with other operations in other towns, they felt that there would be no problems so long as they kept their clients and employees away from their residence. They engaged the Solicitor to review the city's zoning by-law and found that this arrangement complies with the by-laws. While business has not been great, it has been profitable, and the Massage Therapist is generally satisfied with the arrangement. Recent rumours and the actions of Councillor #3 have been of considerable concern to her, as she fears that she might have to give up the business. This, in turn, would mean that she would also have to give up the house, as they could not afford to live in the house without the income from the business.

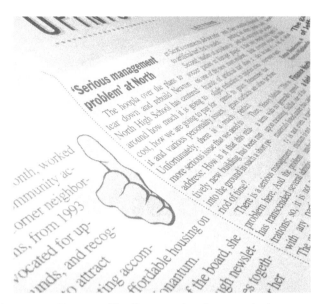

11.24 Newspaper Reporter

Your instructor will play the role of the Newspaper Reporter. The Reporter has been in the business for a long time, but without achieving any real distinction. As a young journalist, the Reporter idolized Bob Woodward of the *Washington Post* (Woodward played a major role in bringing about the downfall of President Richard Nixon) and adopted an aggressive investigative style. In the course of a career that involved working in almost a dozen communities, the Reporter has come to realize that not much really happens in small towns and that investigative reporting can create some powerful adversaries. Generally, the Reporter is cynical about the political process and politicians but still dreams about getting the "big scoop." The Reporter is a very serious person and can usually be found covering council meetings, political events, and meetings of "the great and the good" of the community.

The Reporter lives in a small single-family dwelling in the older part of Summerville (about a block away from the high school). The Reporter is not well paid and does not get a car allowance. Consequently, although the Reporter has a car, it is not used very often. Walking is much cheaper and, as it turns out, is a good way to meet people and find out what is on their minds (which generates leads for new stories). In fact, most people seem to like to enter into discussions with the Reporter in the hope that they might get some tidbit of gossip to repeat to the family at dinner.

11.25 President of the Fire Fighters' Union

The President of the Fire Fighters' Union has been a full-time fire fighter for 15 years. (He served as a volunteer for five years before that.) He has been on the union executive for six years and was elected president last year. His major motivation in seeking the position was to try to do something about health and safety issues. Like many fire fighters, he was concerned about the health risks of exposure to toxic chemicals created when modern materials burn. He is very upset about the Treasurer's attempt to delay acquisition of the replacement breathing equipment.

In his private life, the President is an avid sports fan and family man. Deeply religious, he spends much of his free time assisting with his church's youth programs. Many groups have decried his church's teaching on matters of sexual practice and preference. The President is married, with two sons who are in elementary school. The family has just moved into a split-level house in Royal Heights. His wife is the office manager for a small insurance agency.

11.26
Pub and Motel Owner

The Pub and Motel Owner is very concerned about the highway relocation. While much of the pub's business is derived from local residents who drop in for a drink or a light supper on the way home from work or who spend a long evening out partying, the motel side of the business is dependent on out of town travellers. Most of the units are rented by people who have come to Summerville to work on projects; usually this work relates to the maintenance or installation of equipment at the pulp mills or the sawmills. Business and government officials usually stay at the Summerville Hotel, located downtown, which is a slightly more upscale establishment.

The casino proposal is something of a concern because almost 15 per cent of the pub's profits come from various types of gaming. On the other hand, anything that brings more people into town is bound to enhance the pub and motel business.

11.27 Public Health Inspector

The Public Health Inspector is a provincial civil servant. One of the roles of the Public Health Inspector is to promote improvements in sanitary conditions in the city. The Public Health Department has identified the poor sewage disposal in Riverside Acres as a major problem, and the Health Inspector has been empowered to use whatever moral suasion is necessary to get the city to install a proper community sewage collection system in the area.

11.28 Real Estate Developer

The Real Estate Developer was born and raised in Summerville and has been a real estate agent for many years. In addition to selling real estate, the Real Estate Developer has been responsible for about half of the new commercial buildings constructed over the past fifteen years (not that there have been very many). The Real Estate Developer has been very successful financially and, together with a partner, lives in a very large house on Ridgeview Drive, just north and west of the city boundary. In fact, it could be said that they live on an estate. The Real Estate Developer has vacant land holdings in the downtown, on the highway adjacent to Steamboat Bend, and in the South Bench area (in addition to partial ownership of many of the downtown commercial buildings).

The Real Estate Developer and partner are not very active in community events (they spend much of the winter in Mexico), but they are generous in supporting local teams and charities.

11.29 Ridgeview Drive Resident

The Ridgeview Drive resident and partner are "car nuts." There is nothing they like better than to have their heads under the hood trying to bring an old car back to life. So far, they have restored a 1952 Chevrolet Sedan and are working on restoring a customized 1949 Mercury. Anticipating retirement, they purchased some vehicles of a more recent vintage, and they intend to restore these cars when they have retired. They selected newer vintage models because these vehicles were not yet classics and were still cheap. They had intended to put the vehicles at the back of the lot, where they have a shop, but the drainage is rather poor there and the ground proved to be too muddy. Their lot is almost 1 hectare, with lots of room in the front, so they lined the vehicles up along the road, in full view of their living room window, so that they can keep an eye on the cars. The plan is to build storage sheds (adjacent to their shop) to house the vehicles.

They have two grandchildren (both boys) who live about 2 km down Ridgeview Drive. The boys are in their early teens and have expressed an interest in the cars, and the Ridgeview Drive Resident thinks that it would be a good thing to get the boys involved in restoring the vehicles.

The Ridgeview Drive Resident and partner are incensed that the neighbours think their cars are unsightly. They point out that, with the exception of the Real Estate Agent, none of the residents of Ridgeview Drive have done much to beautify their lots, and they do not see that the cars constitute an eyesore (although the paint is faded on a couple, one has a fender missing, and the other two have rusty chrome).

11.30 Riverside Acres Owner

The Riverside Acres Owner owns (together with other members of the family) eight vacant lots in Riverside Acres. The lots are essentially worthless, as the city has imposed a moratorium on building permits in the area. But family members want to have the moratorium lifted or to have the city install sewers, so they can sell the lots. They have decided that their first tactic should be to ask to get a building permit. If they cannot get that, they will make a proposal to the city to have a sewer system installed. If they are unsuccessful in this effort, they will try to get the city to reconsider the moratorium (but they recognize that this last goal will be difficult given the views of the regional health authority's chief medical officer.) The Riverside Acres Owner has been designated to speak on behalf of the family.

11.31 Riverside Anglican Church Minister

The Minister has lived in Summerville for over a decade and is a very popular figure in the community. The Minister serves a small congregation in an historic log church located at the intersection of Ninth Avenue and Valley Drive (across from the elementary school). The Minister is quite liberal minded and has willingly and publicly supported many groups involved in various social issues, including the Gay Pride Day Committee. (In fact, the Minister serves as co-chair of this committee). The Minister's spouse is a loans officer at a local branch of a major chartered bank. They have no children and live in a small house in the older part of town. While they have been active in supporting groups and individuals that they consider "disadvantaged" or "underdogs," the Minister is uncompromising on matters of faith. The Minister is also somewhat of a local historian and opposes the destruction or relocation of Summerville's historic buildings.

11.32 Royal Heights Resident

The Royal Heights Resident is the leader of the group that submitted the letter to city council protesting about the wild flower garden. A long-time resident of the area, the Royal Heights Resident lives about two blocks from the Wild Flower Lady and is supported in the protest by the Wild Flower Lady's neighbour and two other inhabitants of the area.

Nearing retirement, the Royal Heights Resident and partner are very proud of their house and the neighbourhood. It is, in their words, "What a residential area should look like ... with manicured lawns and flower beds and magnificent trees." They are concerned that any deviation from the pattern will result in a decline in the value of the homes. They are counting on their investment in their house to finance a move to some type of condominium or apartment when they grow too old to live in their own home.

They believe that council should act to protect their property values. They also believe that if someone wants a different or "alternative" lifestyle, then that person should move.

11.33
Solicitor

The Solicitor has a general legal practice in Summerville. The majority of the legal work is related to families and real estate. A significant portion of the income comes from representing individuals who feel that they do not have the required negotiating or speaking skills to represent themselves. The Solicitor is also intimately involved in the proposal to construct "big box" retail stores on the east bench, and is a member of the Riverside Anglican Church Board of Directors.

11.34
Speedy Taxi Driver

At 52 years old, with a grade 7 education, two children, no spouse, and a leg injury from a car accident 15 years ago, Speedy Taxi Driver does not see any career prospects other than driving a taxi. Sure, speeding has been an issue, but with rising gas prices the pressure to go fast to fit in more trips is enormous. Besides, when you drive ten hours a day, there is bound to be the odd time when you slip over the speed limit. Everyone does it, and it is unfair to single out taxi drivers for special attention. At least, that is what Speedy Taxi Driver thinks.

Speedy Taxi Driver is proud of a ten-year accident-free record. Drinking is a bit of a problem, but, by being very careful never to drink within eight hours of starting the next driving shift, Speedy Taxi Driver has never had a brush with the law over impaired driving. Being drunk in the pub—sure. Drunk driving—no way.

Frankly, Speedy Taxi Driver is very confused about the whole licence suspension issue and is very concerned about having to go to a council meeting. Conversations with the police and the City Clerk have not given Speedy Taxi Driver any clear indication of what to expect, or how to prepare a defence.

11.35
Sports Parent

The Sports Parent has two sons and one daughter, all of whom are very active in sports. The daughter plays on the junior girls' volleyball teams at the local high school and will advance to the senior team next year. She also plays soccer in summer. The two boys are involved in minor hockey, soccer, and cross-country running. Most of the Sports Parent's spare time is spent transporting children to games, participating in committee meetings, attending games, and raising funds for team trips. The Sports Parent also works full time (at the pulp mill), as does the Sports Parent's partner. They live in Emerald Estates.

11.36 Wild Flower Lady

The Wild Flower Lady is a resident of Royal Heights. She is an avid gardener and an even more avid environmentalist. Among her concerns are recycling, the introduction of chemicals into the ground water, and water conservation. She has become very concerned about the long-term effects of trying to maintain a lush green lawn. As a result, she determined that she would "do something." In the end, she took out her green lawn (which had been the envy of the neighbourhood) and planted a "natural" garden that did not require watering or fertilizing. It consists mainly of grasses and wild flowers that are, at some times of the year, very beautiful but that are, at other times, somewhat scraggly. She knows that her neighbours are not impressed and has had several heated discussions with them about the matter.

She has not been on good terms with the neighbours next to her house because their cats constantly use her backyard vegetable garden and their dog has frequently planted bones in her front-yard flowerbeds. She has also had friction with the neighbours to the rear, as she has planted some lilies along the rear fence, and these flowers aggravate the neighbour's allergies.

Despite these frictions, the Wild Flower Lady has given generously of her time to help many of her neighbours develop their vegetable gardens and flowerbeds by providing cuttings, compost, and useful advice (and even a bit of labour).

The Wildflower Lady is Councillor #5's aunt.

TWELVE
The Election

This section of the workbook explains the legislation that governs the election of members of council in Summerville and the procedures for nominating members of council and the mayor. It also describes the eligible voters and the rules for conducting the election. The City Clerk will use this information to plan and conduct the election to fill the office of mayor and to fill any vacancies on council (some members of council may want to resign in order to stand for election as mayor).

In some Canadian municipalities, councillors are elected "at large." This means that they are elected in a general vote of all eligible voters in a municipality and, once elected, are responsible for representing all citizens in this municipality. Council elections in other Canadian municipalities, however, are organized according to the ward system. Councillors run for office in particular "wards"—defined districts within a municipality. In this case, only citizens living within the boundaries of the ward are eligible to vote for the candidates running for office in that ward, and, once elected, the councillor is primarily responsible for representing the interests of his or her ward.

In Summerville, council elections can take place using either the "at large" system or the ward system. In the case of the former, councillors will be elected by all the citizens of Summerville and will be responsible for representing the whole municipality (not particular parts). In the case of the latter, the number of wards will depend on the number of participants. Your instructor will tell you if the ward system will be used, and if so, how the wards are structured.

12.1 Election Legislation

This section of the workbook contains extracts from the election legislation applicable to Summerville (which is set out in the *Municipal Government Act*, which is an act of the provincial legislature). All members of the simulation are eligible voters, and there are no other eligible voters in Summerville. The list of electors is the list of participants. All participants are eligible to hold office, unless the legislation specifically says otherwise.

Extracts from the MUNICIPAL GOVERNMENT ACT

ELECTIONS
By-elections
290 (1) Subject to this section, an election must be held to fill a vacancy in an elected local government office that occurs in any of the following circumstances:
a) the person elected or appointed to the office dies before taking office;
b) the office is declared vacant on an application to the courts or a candidate affected by the application renounces claim to the office;
c) the person holding the office dies;
d) the person holding the office resigns from office;
e) the office becomes vacant because the person holding the office has been disqualified from holding the office.

(2) The chief election officer must set a general voting day for the election, which must be no later than 120 days after the date the chief election officer was appointed.

(3) A person elected in a by-election holds office until the end of the term of the office in respect of which the election was held.

Appointment of election officials
291 For the purposes of conducting an election, the City Clerk shall be deemed to be the chief election officer.

Chief election officer duties and powers
292 (1) In addition to all other duties established by this Part, the chief election officer must do the following:

a) ensure that a sufficient number of ballots are prepared for an election by voting,

b) take all reasonable precautions to ensure that a person does not vote more than once in an election,

c) do all other things necessary for the conduct of an election in accordance with this Part and any regulations and by-laws under this Part.

Keeping order at election proceedings
293 A presiding election official must maintain peace and order so far as reasonably possible at the election proceedings for which the presiding election official is responsible.

Disqualification of local government employees
297 (1) For the purposes of this section, "employee" means an employee or salaried officer of a municipality.

(2) Unless the requirements of this section are met, an employee of a municipality is disqualified from being nominated for, being elected to, or holding office as a member of the council of the municipality.

(3) Before being nominated for an office to which subsection (2) or (3) applies, the employee must give notice in writing to his or her employer of the employee's intention to consent to nomination.

(4) Once notice is given under subsection (3), the employee is entitled to and must take a leave of absence from the employee's position with the employer for a period that, at a minimum,

a) begins on the first day of the nomination period or the date on which the notice is given, whichever is later, and

b) ends, as applicable,
   i) if the person is not nominated before the end of the nomination period, on the day after the end of that period;
   ii) if the person withdraws as a candidate in the election, on the day after the withdrawal;
   iii) if the person is declared elected, on the day the person resigns in accordance with subsection (8);
   iv) if the person is not declared elected, on the date when the results of the election are determined.

(6) Before making the oath of office, an employee on a leave of absence under this section who has been elected must resign from the person's position with the employer.

Only one elected office at a time in the same local government
298 (1) At any one time, a person may not hold more than one elected office in the same local government.

(2) At any one time, a person may not be nominated for more than one elected office in the same local government.

(3) A current member of a local government may not be nominated for an election for another office in the same local government unless the person resigns from office before being nominated for the said office.

NOMINATING MEMBERS OF COUNCIL AND THE MAYOR
Summerville operates under special legislation (the *Summerville Nomination and Elections Act*) governing the nomination and election procedures to be used in by-elections. The relevant sections of the special legislation are set out below.

Nomination period
6 The period for receiving nominations to fill a vacancy on the council ends at the end of the council meeting immediately before the council meeting at which the election will be held, except that, in the case of a member of council wishing to be nominated for the office of mayor, the period for receiving nominations to fill the office of mayor ends at the end of the second council meeting before the council meeting at which the election will be held.

Who may make nominations
7 (1) A nomination for office as a member of a local government must be made in writing by two persons who are electors.

(2) Each person nominated must be nominated by separate nomination documents, but a person entitled to make a nomination may subscribe to as many nomination documents as there are per-

sons to be elected to fill the office for which the election is being held.

Nomination documents

8 (1) A nomination for local government office must be in written form and must include the following:
a) the full name or usual name of the person nominated;
b) the office for which the person is nominated;
c) the names of the nominators.

(2) A nomination must be accompanied by the following:
a) a statement signed by the person nominated
   i) consenting to the nomination
   ii) confirming that he or she is qualified to be nominated for the office.

(3) The chief election officer may require a person nominated to provide a telephone number at which the person may be contacted.

Nomination by delivery of nomination documents

9 (1) Nomination documents must be received before the end of the nomination period by the chief election officer.

(2) The obligation to ensure that the nomination documents are received in accordance with this section rests with the person being nominated.

(3) Nomination documents must be delivered by hand.

Declaration of candidates

10 Immediately following the end of the nomination period, the chief election officer must declare as candidates for an elected office all persons who have been nominated for the office.

Declaration of election by voting or acclamation

11 (1) If there are more candidates for an office than there are to be elected for the office, the chief election officer must declare that an election by voting is to be held.

(2) If no more candidates for an office are nominated than there are to be elected for that office, the chief election officer must declare the candidate or candidates elected by acclamation.

Appointment if an insufficient number of candidates are elected

12 If there are fewer candidates declared elected by acclamation than there are positions to be elected, the instructor must appoint a person to each vacant office.

CONDUCTING THE ELECTION

Summerville also has special legislation governing the conduct of elections. While it is similar to the legislation applicable to other municipalities, it does have unique features. All members of the class are citizens of Summerville and therefore are entitled to vote at the election. Summerville's legislation is as follows:

Voting opportunities for electors

15 An elector who meets the applicable qualifications may vote in an election.

Required general voting opportunities

16 The voting places under subsection (1) must be opened on general voting day from a time designated by the chief election officer and must remain open until all electors have cast their ballots, or for fifteen minutes, whichever is less.

Required advance voting opportunities

17 There is no requirement to provide advance voting.

Form of ballots

18 The chief election officer must establish the form of ballots to be used in an election.

What may be included on a ballot

19 A ballot for an election may include the following:
a) instructions as to the number of candidates to be elected to the office;
b) instructions as to the appropriate mark that registers a valid vote for a candidate;
c) the full name of each candidate or, if a candidate specified a different usual name in the nomination documents, this usual name.

What must not be included on a ballot

20 A ballot for an election must not include any of the following:
a) an indication that a candidate is holding or has held an elected office;

b) a candidate's occupation;

c) an indication of a title, honour, degree, or decoration received or held by a candidate.

Order of names on ballot

21 (1) On the ballot,

a) the names of the candidates must be arranged alphabetically by their surnames, and

b) if two or more candidates have the same surname, the names of those candidates must be arranged alphabetically in order of their first given names.

(2) The chief election officer's decision on the order of names on a ballot is final.

Ballot boxes

22 Ballot boxes for an election may be any box or other appropriate receptacle.

Voting to be by secret ballot

23 (1) Voting at an election must be by secret ballot.

(2) Each person present at a place at which an elector exercises the right to vote, including persons present to vote, and each person present at the counting of the vote must preserve the secrecy of the ballot and, in particular, must not do any of the following:

a) interfere with a person who is marking a ballot;

b) attempt to discover how another person voted;

c) communicate information regarding how another person voted or marked a ballot;

d) induce a person, directly or indirectly, to show a ballot in a way that reveals how the person voted.

Each elector may vote only once

24 A person must not vote more than once in the same election.

Replacement of spoiled ballot

25 If an elector unintentionally spoils a ballot before it is deposited in a ballot box, the elector may obtain a replacement ballot by giving the spoiled ballot to the presiding election official.

How to vote by ballot

26 (1) After receiving a ballot, an elector must

a) proceed without delay to a voting compartment provided;

b) while the ballot is screened from observation, mark it by making a cross in the blank space opposite the name of the candidate or candidates for whom the elector wishes to vote;

c) fold the ballot to conceal all marks made on it by the elector;

d) leave the voting compartment without delay;

e) deposit the ballot in the appropriate sealed ballot box;

f) leave the voting place without delay.

(2) An election official may and, if requested by the elector, must explain to an elector the proper method for voting by ballot.

When and where counting is to be done

27 The counting of the votes on ballots for an election must not take place until the close of voting for the election, but must take place as soon as possible after this time.

Who may be present at counting

28 A presiding election official and at least one other election official must be present while counting proceedings are being conducted.

Who does the counting

29 The counting of the votes on ballots for an election must be conducted by the presiding election official or by other election officials under the supervision of the presiding election official.

Procedures for counting

30 (1) All ballots in each ballot box must be considered in accordance with this section.

(2) As each ballot for an election is considered, it must be placed in such a manner that the persons present at the counting are able to see how the ballot is marked.

(3) Unless rejected under section 31 (4), a mark referred to in section 31 (1) on a ballot for an election must be accepted and counted as a valid vote.

(4) Counting must proceed as continuously as is practicable, and the votes must be recorded.

(5) The presiding election official must endorse ballots to indicate the following as applicable:
a) that the ballot was rejected under section 31 in relation to an election.

(6) An endorsement under subsection (5) must be made at the time the presiding election official considers the ballot and in such a manner that it does not alter or obscure the elector's marking on the ballot.

Rules for accepting votes and rejecting ballots
31 (1) The following are marks that are to be accepted and counted as valid votes for an election unless the ballot is rejected under subsection (4):
a) a mark of the type required by section 26 (1) (b);
b) a tick mark that is placed in the location required by section 26 (1) (b);
c) a mark of the type required by section 26 (1) (b) that is out of or partly out of the location on the ballot in which it is required to be put by that provision, as long as the mark is placed in such a manner as to indicate clearly the intent of the elector to vote for a particular candidate;
d) a tick mark that is placed as described in paragraph (c).

(2) A mark on a ballot other than a mark referred to in subsection (1) must not be accepted and counted as a valid vote.

(3) Ballots must be rejected as invalid in accordance with the following:
a) a ballot must be rejected in total if it appears that the ballot physically differs from the ballots provided by the chief election officer for the election;
b) a ballot must be rejected in total if there are no marks referred to in subsection (1) on it;
c) a ballot must be rejected in total if the ballot is uniquely marked, or otherwise uniquely dealt with, in such a manner that the elector could reasonably be identified;
d) a ballot must be rejected in total if more than one form of mark referred to in subsection (1) is on the ballot;

e) a ballot is to be rejected in relation to an election if there are more marks referred to in subsection (1) for the election on the ballot than there are candidates to be elected.

Ballot account
32 (1) Once all counting at a place is completed, ballot accounts for each election must be prepared in accordance with this section and signed by the presiding election official.

(2) A ballot account must include the following:
a) the office to be filled by the election
b) the number of valid votes for each candidate in the election.

Declaration of official election results
33 (1) Upon completion of the counting of the ballots, the chief election officer must declare the results of the election.

(2) If a candidate cannot be declared elected because there is an equality of valid votes for two or more candidates, the chief election officer must toss a coin to determine which candidate is to be declared elected. The coin toss must be performed before the citizens of Summerville.

When elected candidates may take office
34 A candidate declared elected under section 33 takes office as soon as the results of the election are declared.

Vote buying and intimidation
435 (1) In this section, "inducement" includes money, gift, valuable consideration, refreshment, entertainment, office, placement, employment, and any other benefit of any kind.

(2) A person must not intimidate or pay, give, lend, or procure inducement for any of the following purposes:
a) to induce a person to vote or refrain from voting;
b) to induce a person to vote or refrain from voting for or against a particular candidate;
c) to reward a person for having voted or refrained from voting as described in paragraph (a) or (b);

d) to procure or induce a person to attempt to procure the election of a particular candidate, the defeat of a particular candidate, or a particular result in an election;

e) to procure or induce a person to attempt to procure the vote of an elector or the failure of an elector to vote.

(3) A person must not accept inducement to do any of the actions enumerated in section (2).

APPENDIX I

This appendix includes extracts of the Summerville City Council's procedure by-law. Some provisions (which have been judged to be not relevant for the simulation) have been omitted for the sake of brevity. These omissions account for the missing sections of the by-law.

COUNCIL PROCEDURE BY-LAW A BY-LAW OF THE CITY OF SUMMERVILLE

The Municipal Council of the City of Summerville enacts as follows:

PART 1: INTRODUCTION

Title
1) This by-law may be cited as the "COUNCIL PROCEDURE BY-LAW NO. 1742, 2001."

Definitions
2) In this by-law:
"City" means the City of Summerville
"committee" means a standing, select, or other committee of Council, but does not include COTW
"COTW" means the Committee of the Whole Council
 "Council" means the Council of the City of Summerville

Application of rules of procedure
3) The provisions of this by-law govern the proceedings of Council, COTW, and all standing and select committees of Council, as applicable.

4) In cases not provided for under this by-law, *The New Robert's Rules of Order*, 2nd edition, 1998, apply to the proceedings of Council, COTW, and Council committees.

PART 3: DESIGNATION OF MEMBER TO ACT IN PLACE OF MAYOR

7) Annually Council must from amongst its members designate councillors to serve on a rotating basis as the member responsible for acting in the place of the mayor when the mayor is absent or otherwise unable to act.

8) The member chosen under section 9 has the same powers and duties as the mayor in relation to the applicable matter.

9) When the office of mayor is vacant due to the death, resignation, or disqualification of the incumbent, the Council members shall, within 21 days of the death, resignation, or disqualification of the mayor, choose a councillor to act as mayor until such time as a mayor may be elected by by-election or at a general election.

PART 4: COUNCIL PROCEEDINGS

Attendance of Public at Meetings
10) Except where the provisions of section 12 apply, all Council meetings must be open to the public.

11) The Council must not vote on the reading or adoption of a by-law when a meeting is closed to the public.

12) A part of a Council meeting may be closed to the public if the subject matter being considered relates to or is one or more of the following:
a) Personal information about an identifiable individual who holds or is being considered for a position as an officer, employee, or agent of the municipality or another position appointed by the municipality;
b) Labour relations or other employee relations;
c) The security of the property of the municipality;
d) The acquisition, disposition, or expropriation of land or improvements, if the Council considers that disclosure could reasonably be expected to harm the interests of the municipality;

e) Law enforcement, if the Council considers that disclosure could reasonably be expected to harm the conduct of an investigation under or enforcement of an enactment;

f) Litigation or potential litigation affecting the municipality;

g) The receipt of advice that is subject to solicitor-client privilege, including communications necessary for that purpose;

h) Negotiations and related discussions respecting the proposed provision of a municipal service that are at their preliminary stages and that, in the view of the Council, could reasonably be expected to harm the interests of the municipality if they were held in public.

i) Discussions with municipal officers and employees respecting municipal objectives, measures, and progress reports for the purposes of preparing an annual report;

j) The consideration of whether a Council meeting should be closed.

13) Before closing a Council meeting or part of a Council meeting to the public, Council must, by resolution, state the fact that the meeting or part of the meeting is to be closed and the basis under section 12 on which the meeting is to be closed.

14) Sections 12 and 13 also apply to meetings of Council committees, municipal commissions, and any advisory body or review panel established by Council.

Minutes of meetings to be maintained and available to public

15) Minutes of the proceedings of Council must be
a) legibly recorded,
b) certified as correct by the city clerk, and
c) signed by the mayor or other member presiding at the meeting or at the next meeting at which the minutes are adopted.

16) Subject to section 17, minutes of the proceedings of Council must be open for public inspection at city hall during its regular office hours.

17) Section 16 does not apply to minutes of a Council meeting or that part of a Council meeting from which persons were excluded under section 12.

Calling meeting to order

18) As soon as there is a quorum present, after the time specified for a Council meeting, the mayor, if present, must take the Chair and call the Council meeting to order. When the mayor is absent, however, the councillor designated as the member responsible for acting in the place of the mayor in accordance with section 9 must take the Chair and call such meeting to order.

Agenda

19) Prior to each Council meeting, the city clerk must prepare an agenda setting out all the items for consideration at that meeting, noting in short form a summary for each item on the agenda.

20) Council must not consider any matters not listed on the agenda unless a new matter for consideration is properly introduced as a late item pursuant to section 23.

Order of proceedings and business

21) The agenda for all regular Council meetings contains the following matters in the order in which they are listed below:
a) Approval of agenda;
b) Adoption of minutes;
c) Introduction of late items;
d) Public and statutory hearings, and third reading or adoption of by-laws where applicable after each hearing;
e) Delegations—requests to address Council;
f) Report of chief administrative officer;
g) Unfinished business;
h) Correspondence;
i) Reports of committees, COTW, and commissions;
j) Resolutions;
k) By-laws;
l) Question period;
m) New business; and
n) Adjournment.

22) Particular business at a Council meeting must, in all cases, be taken up in the order in which it is listed on the agenda unless otherwise resolved by Council.

Late items

23) An item of business not included on the agenda must not be considered at a Council meeting unless introduction of the late item is approved by Council at the time allocated on the agenda for such matters.

24) If the Council makes a resolution under section 23, information pertaining to late items must be distributed to the members.

Voting at meetings

25) The following procedures apply to voting at Council meetings:

a) When debate on a matter is closed, the presiding member must put the matter to a vote of Council members.

b) When the Council is ready to vote, the presiding member must put the matter to a vote by stating "Those in favour raise your hands" and then "Those opposed raise your hands."

c) When the presiding member is putting the matter to a vote under paragraphs (a) and (b) a member must not:

i) cross or leave the room,

ii) make a noise or other disturbance, or

iii) interrupt the voting procedure under paragraph (b) unless the interrupting member is raising a point of order.

d) After the presiding member finally puts the question to a vote under paragraph (b), a member must not speak to the question or make a motion concerning it.

e) The presiding member's decision about whether a question has been finally put is conclusive.

f) Whenever a vote of Council on a matter is taken, each member present shall signify a vote by raising a hand, and the presiding member must declare the result of the voting by stating that the question is decided in either the affirmative or the negative.

Delegations

26) The Council may, by resolution, allow an individual or a delegation to address Council at a meeting on the subject of an agenda item provided written application has been received by the city clerk prior to preparation of the agenda for the meeting. Each address must be limited to five minutes unless a longer period is agreed to by unanimous vote of those members present.

27) Where written application has not been received by the city clerk, as prescribed in section 26, an individual or delegation may address the meeting if approved by the unanimous vote of the members present.

28) Council must not permit a delegation to address a meeting of the Council regarding a by-law in respect of which a public hearing has been held, where the public hearing is required under an enactment as a prerequisite to the adoption of the by-law.

29) The city clerk may schedule delegations to another Council meeting or advisory body as deemed appropriate according to the subject matter of the delegation.

30) The city clerk may refuse to place a delegation on the agenda if the issue is not considered to fall within the jurisdiction of Council. If the delegation wishes to appeal the city clerk's decision, the information must be distributed under separate cover to Council for its consideration.

Conduct and debate

31) A Council member may speak to a question or motion at a Council meeting only if that member first addresses the presiding member.

32) Members must address the presiding member by that person's title of mayor, acting mayor, or councillor.

33) Members must address other non-presiding members by the title councillor.

34) No member must interrupt a member who is speaking except to raise a point of order.

35) If more than one member speaks, the presiding member must call on the member who, in the presiding member's opinion, first spoke.

36) Members who are called to order by the presiding member must immediately stop speaking, may explain their position on the point of order, and may appeal to Council for its decision on the point of order.

37) Members speaking at a Council meeting

a) must use respectful language,

b) must not use offensive gestures or signs,

c) must speak only in connection with the matter being debated, and may speak about a vote of Council only for the purpose of making a motion that the vote be rescinded; and

d) must adhere to the rules of procedure established under this by-law and to the decisions of the presiding member and Council in connection with the rules and points of order.

38) If a member does not adhere to section 37, the presiding member may order the member to leave the member's seat, and

a) if the member refuses to leave, the presiding member may cause the member to be removed from the member's seat by a peace officer, and

b) if the member apologizes to the Council, Council may, by resolution, allow the member to retake the member's seat.

39) A member may require the question being debated at a Council meeting to be read at any time during the debate if that does not interrupt another member who is speaking.

40) The following rules apply to limit speech on matters being considered at a Council meeting:

a) a member may speak more than once in connection with the same question only with the permission of Council, or if the member is explaining a material part of a previous speech without introducing a new matter;

b) a member who has made a substantive motion to the Council may reply to the debate;

c) a member who has moved an amendment, the previous question, or an instruction to a committee may not reply to the debate;

d) a member may speak to a question, or may speak in reply, for longer than a total time of five minutes only with the permission of Council.

Motions generally

41) Council may debate and vote on a motion only if it is first made by one Council member and then seconded by another.

42) A motion that deals with a matter that is not on the agenda of the Council meeting at which the motion is introduced may be introduced with Council's permission.

43) A Council member may make only the following motions, when the Council is considering a question:

a) to refer to committee;

b) to amend;

c) to lay on the table;

d) to postpone indefinitely;

e) to postpone to a certain time;

f) to move the previous question; or

g) to adjourn.

44) A motion made under section 43 is not amendable or debatable.

45) Council must vote separately on each distinct part of a question that is under consideration at a Council meeting if requested by a Council member.

Motion to commit

46) Until it is decided, a motion made at a Council meeting to refer to committee precludes an amendment of the main question.

Motion for the main question

47) In this section, "main question," in relation to a matter, means the motion that first brings the matter before the Council.

48) At a Council meeting, the following rules apply to a motion for the main question, or for the main question as amended:

a) if a member of Council moves to put the main question, or the main question as amended, to a vote, that motion must be dealt with before any other amendments are made to the motion on the main question; and

b) if the motion for the main question, or for the main question as amended, is decided in the negative, the Council may again debate the question, or proceed to other business.

Amendments generally

49) A Council member may, without notice, move to amend a motion that is being considered at a Council meeting.

50) A proposed amendment must be reproduced in writing by the mover if requested by the presiding member.

51) A proposed amendment must be decided or withdrawn before the motion being considered is put to a vote unless there is a call for the main question.

52) An amendment may be amended once only.

53) An amendment that has been negated by a vote of Council cannot be proposed again.

54) A Council member may propose an amendment to an adopted amendment.

55) The presiding member must put the main question and its amendments in the following order for the vote of Council:
a) a motion to amend a motion amending the main question;
b) a motion to amend the main question, or an amended motion amending the main question if the vote under subparagraph (a) is positive; and
c) the main question.

Reconsideration by Council member

61) Subject to section 65, a Council member may, at the next Council meeting,
a) move to reconsider a matter on which a vote, other than to postpone indefinitely, has been taken, and
b) move to reconsider an adopted by-law after an interval of at least 24 hours following its adoption.

62) A Council member who voted affirmatively for a resolution adopted by Council may at any time move to rescind that resolution.

63) Council must not discuss the main matter referred to in sections 61 and 62 unless a motion to reconsider that matter is adopted in the affirmative.

64) A vote to reconsider must not be reconsidered.

65) Council may only reconsider a matter that has not
a) had the approval or assent of the electors and been adopted, or
b) been acted on by an officer, employee, or agent of the City.

66) The conditions that applied to the adoption of the original by-law, resolution, or proceeding apply to its rejection under this section.

PART 5: BY-LAW

Reading and adopting by-laws

67) The presiding member of a Council meeting may have the city clerk read a synopsis of each proposed by-law and then request a motion that the proposed by-law be read.

68) A reading of the by-law may be given by stating its title and object.

69) A proposed by-law may be debated and amended at any time during the first three readings.

70) Each reading of a proposed by-law must receive the affirmative vote of a majority of the Council members present.

71) Council may give two or three readings of a proposed by-law at the same Council meeting.

72) Council may adopt a proposed official community plan or zoning by-law at the same meeting at which the plan or by-law passed third reading.

PART 7: COMMITTEE OF THE WHOLE

Going into Committee of the Whole

77) At any time during a Council meeting, Council may by resolution go into COTW.

78) In addition to section 77, a meeting, other than a standing or select committee meeting, to which all members of Council are invited to consider but not to decide on matters of the City's business is a meeting of COTW.

Minutes of COTW meetings to be maintained and available to public

79) Sections 15 to 17 apply to minutes and proceedings of COTW.

Presiding members at COTW meetings and quorum

80) Any Council member may preside in COTW.

81) The members of Council attending a meeting of COTW must appoint a presiding member for the COTW meeting.

82) The quorum of COTW is the majority of Council members.

Points of order at meetings

83) The presiding member must preserve order at a COTW meeting and, subject to an appeal to other members present, decide points of order that may arise.

Conduct and debate

84) The following rules apply to COTW meetings:
a) a motion is not required to be seconded;
b) a motion for adjournment is not allowed;
c) a member may speak any number of times on the same question; and
d) a member must not speak longer than a total of five minutes on any one question.

Voting at meetings

85) Votes at a COTW meeting must be taken by a show of hands if requested by a member.

86) The presiding member must declare the results of voting.

Rising without reporting

87) A motion made at a COTW meeting to rise without reporting
a) is always in order and takes precedence over all other motions,
b) may be debated, and
c) may not be addressed more than once by any one member.

88) If a motion to rise without reporting is adopted by COTW at a meeting constituted under section 38(1), the Council meeting must resume and proceed to the next order of business.

PART 8: COMMITTEES

Duties of standing committees

92) Standing committees must consider, inquire into, report, and make recommendations to Council about all of the following matters:
a) matters that are related to the general subject indicated by the name of the committee;
b) matters that are assigned by Council; and
c) matters that are assigned by the mayor.

Minutes of committee meetings to be maintained and available to public

93) Sections 15 to 17 apply to minutes and proceedings of standing committees.

Quorum

94) The quorum for a committee is a majority of all of its members.

Conduct and debate

95) The rules of Council procedure must be observed during committee meetings, so far as is possible and unless as otherwise provided in this by-law.

96) Council members attending a meeting of a committee, of which they are not a member, may participate in the discussion only with the permission of a majority of the committee members present.

97) A motion made at a meeting of a committee is not required to be seconded.

Voting at meetings

98) Council members attending a meeting of a committee of which they are not a member must not vote on a question.

APPENDIX 2

Legislative Extracts

The following extracts from the *Municipal Government Act* are applicable to the City of Summerville and are provided for the assistance of participants in the simulation. Gaps in numbering are the result of omission of provisions that were not deemed to be applicable to the simulation.

Purposes and Powers

MUNICIPALITIES AND THEIR COUNCILS

1) A municipality is a corporation of the residents of its area.

2) The governing body of a municipality is its council.

MUNICIPAL PURPOSES

3) The purposes of a municipality include
   a) providing for good government of its community;
   b) providing for services, laws, and other matters for community benefit;
   c) providing for stewardship of the public assets of its community; and
   d) fostering the economic, social, and environmental well-being of its community.

FUNDAMENTAL POWERS

4) A municipality has the capacity, rights, powers, and privileges of a natural person of full capacity.

5) A municipality may provide any service that the council considers necessary or desirable, and it may do this directly or through another public authority or another person or organization.

6) A council may, by by-law, regulate, prohibit, and impose requirements in relation to the following:
   a) municipal services;
   b) public places;
   c) trees;
   d) firecrackers, fireworks, and explosives;
   e) bows and arrows, knives, and other weapons not referred to in subsection (5);
   f) cemeteries, crematoriums, columbariums, and mausoleums and the interment or other disposition of the dead;
   g) the health, safety, or protection of persons or of property in relation to the protection of persons and property;
   h) the protection and enhancement of the well-being of its community in relation to nuisances, disturbances, and other objectionable situations;
   i) public health;
   j) protection of the natural environment;
   k) animals;
   l) buildings and other structures;
   m) the removal of soil and the deposit of soil or other material.

7) A council may, by by-law, regulate and impose requirements in relation to signs and other advertising.

8) A council may, by by-law, regulate and prohibit in relation to the discharge of firearms.

9) A council may, by by-law, regulate in relation to business.

10) The powers under sections (4) to (9) to regulate, prohibit, and impose requirements, as applicable, in relation to a matter are separate powers that may be exercised independently of one another, and include the power to regulate, prohibit, and impose requirements, as applicable, respecting persons, property, things, and activities in relation to the matter.

11) As examples, the powers to regulate, prohibit, and impose requirements under this section include the following powers:
    a) to provide that persons may engage in a regulated activity only in accordance with the rules established by by-law;
    b) to prohibit persons from doing things with their property;

c) to require persons to do things with their property, to do things at their expense, and to provide security for fulfilling a requirement.

12) A municipality must make available to the public, on request, a statement respecting the council's reasons for adopting a by-law under sections 4 to 9.

Division 2—Scope of Jurisdiction

RELATIONSHIP WITH PROVINCIAL LAWS

16) A provision of a municipal by-law has no effect if it is inconsistent with a provincial enactment.

17) For the purposes of section 16, unless otherwise provided, a municipal by-law is not inconsistent with another enactment if a person who complies with the by-law does not, by this, contravene the other enactment.

SERVICES OUTSIDE THE MUNICIPALITY

18) A municipality may provide a service in an area outside the municipality, but it must first obtain consent as follows:
   a) if the area is in another municipality, the council must obtain the consent of the council of the other municipality;
   b) if the area is not in another municipality, the council must obtain the consent of the regional government board for the area.

19) In giving consent under section 18, the other local government may establish terms and conditions.

LICENSING AND STANDARDS AUTHORITY

22) A council may provide for a system of licences, permits, or approvals, including by doing one or more of the following:
   a) prohibiting any activity or thing until a licence, permit, or approval has been granted;
   b) providing for the granting and refusal of licences, permits, and approvals;
   c) providing for the effective periods of licences, permits, and approvals;
   d) providing for the suspension or cancellation of licences, permits, and approvals for failure to comply with terms or condi-

tions or by-laws applicable to the license or permit;
   e) providing for reconsideration or appeals of decisions made with respect to the granting, refusal, suspension, or cancellation of licences, permits, and approvals.

Financial Management

FISCAL YEAR

32) The fiscal year for a municipality is the calendar year.

FINANCIAL PLAN

35) A municipality must have a financial plan that is adopted annually, by by-law, before the annual property tax by-law is adopted.

36) For certainty, the financial plan may be amended by by-law at any time.

37) The planning period for a financial plan is five years, that period being the year in which the plan is specified to come into force and the following four years.

38) The financial plan must set out the following for each year of the planning period:
   a) the proposed expenditures by the municipality,
   b) the proposed funding sources,
   c) the proposed transfers to or between funds.

39) The total of the proposed expenditures and transfers to other funds for a year must not exceed the total of the proposed funding sources and transfers from other funds for the year.

40) The proposed expenditures must set out separate amounts for each of the following as applicable:
   a) the amount required to pay interest and principal on municipal debt,
   b) the amount required for capital purposes,
   c) the amount required for a deficiency referred to in subsection (9),
   d) the amount required for other municipal purposes.

41) The proposed funding sources must set out separate amounts for each of the following as applicable:
   a) revenue from property value taxes;
   b) revenue from parcel taxes;

c) revenue from fees;

d) revenue from other sources;

e) proceeds from borrowing, other than borrowing under section 68.

42) The proposed transfers to or between funds must set out separate amounts for

a) each reserve fund under Division 4 of this Part, and

b) accumulated surplus.

43) If actual expenditures and transfers to other funds for a year exceed actual revenues and transfers from other funds for the year, the resulting deficiency must be included in the next year's financial plan as an expenditure in that year.

PUBLIC PROCESS FOR DEVELOPMENT OF THE FINANCIAL PLAN

44) A council must undertake a process of public consultation regarding the proposed financial plan before it is adopted.

Division 3 — Expenditures, Liabilities, and Investments

LIMIT ON EXPENDITURES

51) A municipality must not make an expenditure other than one authorized under section 52 or 53.

52) A municipality may make an expenditure that is included for that year in its financial plan, so long as the expenditure is not expressly prohibited by or under this or another Act.

53) A municipality may make an expenditure for an emergency that was not contemplated for that year in its financial plan, so long as the expenditure is not expressly prohibited by or under this or another Act.

LIMIT ON BORROWING AND OTHER LIABILITIES

54) A municipality may only incur a liability as expressly authorized by or under this or another Act.

55) A municipality may not incur a liability if incurring the liability would cause the municipality to exceed a limit established under section 56 unless this liability is approved under subsection 57.

56) For the purposes of subsection (2), the Lieutenant Governor in Council may make regulations

a) establishing a limit on the aggregate liabilities and the method for determining that limit, and

b) establishing a limit on the annual cost of servicing the aggregate liabilities and the method for determining that limit.

57) With the approval of the inspector, a municipality may exceed the limit established under subsection (3).

58) Except for borrowing under section 68, a municipality must not incur a liability for which expenditures are required during the planning period for its financial plan, unless those expenditures are included for the applicable year in the financial plan.

LIABILITIES UNDER AGREEMENTS

62) A council may, under an agreement, incur a liability if

a) the liability is not a debenture debt, and

b) the period of the liability is not longer than the reasonable life expectancy of the activity, work, or service under the agreement.

63) Subject to sections 65 and 66, if an agreement under section 62 is

a) for more than five years, or

b) for a period that could exceed five years by exercising rights of renewal or extension, the council may only incur the liability with the approval of the electors.

64) The matter put before the electors under section 63 must identify the other parties to the agreement and the nature, term, and amount of the liability.

65) Approval of the electors is not required under section 63 for the following:

a) a liability to be incurred under an employment contract or collective agreement;

b) a liability to be incurred for the supply of materials, equipment, or services under an agreement referred to in section 3 of the *Police Act*.

66) If

a) the concept for a partnering agreement has received the approval of the electors, and

b) within 5 years after that approval, the municipality enters into a partnering agreement that is in accordance with that approved concept, approval under subsection 63 is not required for the partnering agreement.

67) For the purposes of subsection 63, the concept for the agreement to be put before the electors must identify the following:

a) the nature of the activity, work, or facility to be provided under the partnering agreement;

b) the maximum term of the agreement;

c) the maximum liability that may be incurred by the municipality under the agreement;

d) any other information required by regulation.

REVENUE ANTICIPATION BORROWING

68) A council may, by by-law, provide for the borrowing of money that may be necessary to

a) meet current lawful expenditures, and

b) pay amounts required to meet the municipality's taxing obligations in relation to another local government or other public body.

69) When collected, revenue from property taxes must be used as necessary to repay money borrowed under this section.

LOAN AUTHORIZATION BY-LAWS FOR LONG-TERM BORROWING

70) A council may, by a loan authorization by-law adopted with the approval of the inspector, incur a liability by borrowing for one or more of the following:

a) any purpose of a capital nature;

b) lending to any person or public authority under an agreement;

c) guaranteeing repayment of the borrowing, or providing security for the borrowing, of a person or public authority, if this is provided under an agreement with the person or public authority;

d) complying with an order or requirement to pay money into the Supreme Court as security

i) for payment of a judgement or other debt,

ii) for damages or costs, or

iii) for the costs of an appeal from the decision of a court or an arbitrator;

e) satisfying a judgement or other order of a court against the municipality;

f) satisfying an award resulting from an arbitrator's determination of liability or quantum of damages against the municipality, including orders of the arbitrator related to that determination;

g) paying compensation in respect of property expropriated or injured.

71) A loan authorization by-law must set out the following:

a) the total amount proposed to be borrowed under the by-law;

b) in brief and general terms, each of the purposes for which the debt is to be incurred;

c) the amount allocated by the by-law to each of the purposes for which the debt is to be incurred;

d) the maximum term for which the debentures may be issued.

72) A loan authorization by-law may not be included as part of a general by-law.

73) The authority to borrow under a loan authorization by-law ends

a) in the case of a loan authorization by-law under section 70 (b) or (c), at the end of the term of the agreement required by that subsection, and

b) in other cases, five years from the date of adoption of the by-law.

74) The maximum term of a debt that may be authorized by a loan authorization by-law is as follows:

a) in the case of a by-law under section 70 (a), the lesser of

i) 30 years and

ii) the reasonable life expectancy of the capital asset for which the debt is contracted;

b) in the case of a loan authorization by-law under section 70 (b) or (c), the remaining term of the applicable agreement;

c) in all other cases, 30 years.

ELECTOR APPROVAL REQUIRED FOR SOME LOAN AUTHORIZATION BY-LAWS

75) Subject to section 76, a loan authorization by-law may only be adopted with the approval of the electors.

76) Approval of the electors is not required for the following:
   a) money borrowed for a purpose referred to in section 70 (d) to (j)
   b) money borrowed for works required to be carried out under an order for abatement of municipal pollution, environmental protection, or environmental emergency measures provided for in the *Environmental Protection and Management Act*.

INVESTMENT OF MUNICIPAL FUNDS

89) Money held by a municipality that is not immediately required may only be invested or reinvested in one or more of the following:
   a) securities of Canada or of a province;
   b) securities guaranteed for principal and interest by Canada or by a province;
   c) securities of a municipality;
   d) investments guaranteed by a chartered bank;
   e) deposits in a savings institution, or non-equity or membership shares of a credit union;
   f) other investments specifically authorized under this or another act.

OWNERSHIP OF CORPORATIONS

90) A municipality may only
   a) incorporate a corporation other than a society or
   b) acquire shares in a corporation with the approval of the inspector or as authorized by regulation.

91) An incorporation or acquisition under section 90 applies as an exception to the restriction under section 89.

Division 4—Reserve Funds

ESTABLISHMENT OF RESERVE FUNDS

92) A council may, by by-law, establish a reserve fund for a specified purpose and direct that money be placed to the credit of the reserve fund.

USE OF MONEY IN RESERVE FUNDS

93) Subject to this section, money in a reserve fund, and interest earned on it, must be used only for the purpose for which the fund was established.

94) If the amount to the credit of a reserve fund is greater than required for the purpose for which the fund was established, the council may, by by-law, transfer all or part of the amount to another reserve fund.

95) As a restriction on section 94, a transfer from a reserve fund established for a capital purpose may only be made to another reserve fund established for a capital purpose.

Division 5—Restrictions on Use of Municipal Funds

PURPOSES FOR WHICH BORROWED MONEY MAY BE USED

96) Subject to this section, money borrowed by a municipality under any Act must not be used for a purpose other than that specified in the by-law or agreement authorizing the borrowing.

97) If some of the money borrowed for a specified purpose remains unused after payment of the costs related to that purpose, a council may, by by-law, provide for the use of the unused money for one or more of the following:
   a) to retire debentures issued for the purpose;
   b) to purchase and cancel debentures issued for the purpose;
   c) for expenditures of a nature similar to the purpose in the by-law authorizing the money to be borrowed;
   d) for a reserve fund for matters in paragraph (a), (b), or (c).

LIABILITIES FOR USE OF MONEY CONTRARY TO ACT

98) A council member who votes for a by-law or resolution authorizing the expenditure, investment, or other use of money contrary to this Act is personally liable to the municipality for the amount.

99) As an exception, section 98 does not apply if the council member relied on information provided by a municipal officer or employee and the officer or employee was guilty of dishonesty, gross negligence, or malicious or wilful misconduct in relation to the provision of the information.

100) In addition to any other penalty to which the person may be liable, a council member who is liable to the municipality under section 98 is disqualified from holding local government office for a period of 10 years.

101) Money owed to a municipality under this section may be recovered for the municipality by

a) the municipality,

b) an elector or taxpayer of the municipality, or

c) a person who holds a security under a borrowing made by the municipality.

PLANNING AND LAND USE MANAGEMENT

Purposes of official community plans

115) An official community plan is a statement of objectives and policies to guide decisions on planning and land use management, within the area covered by the plan, respecting the purposes of local government.

AUTHORITY TO ADOPT BY BY-LAW

116) A local government may, by by-law, adopt one or more official community plans.

REQUIRED CONTENT

117) An official community plan must include statements and map designations for the area covered by the plan respecting the following:

a) the approximate location, amount, type, and density of residential development required to meet anticipated housing needs over a period of at least five years;

b) the approximate location, amount, and type of present and proposed commercial, industrial, institutional, agricultural, recreational, and public utility land uses;

c) the approximate location and area of sand and gravel deposits that are suitable for future sand and gravel extraction;

d) restrictions on the use of land that is subject to hazardous conditions or that is environmentally sensitive to development;

e) the approximate location and phasing of any major road, sewer, and water systems;

f) the approximate location and type of present and proposed public facilities, including schools, parks, and waste treatment and disposal sites;

g) other matters that may, in respect of any plan, be required or authorized by the minister.

118) An official community plan must include housing policies of the local government respecting affordable housing, rental housing, and special needs housing.

POLICY STATEMENTS IN COMMUNITY PLAN

119) An official community plan may include the following:

a) policies of the local government relating to social needs, social well-being, and social development;

b) a regional context statement;

c) policies of the local government respecting the maintenance and enhancement of farming on land in a farming area or in an area designated for agricultural use in the community plan;

d) policies of the local government relating to the preservation, protection, restoration, and enhancement of the natural environment, its ecosystems and biological diversity.

120) If a local government proposes to include a matter in an official community plan, the regulation of which is not within the jurisdiction of the local government, the plan may only state the broad objective of the local government with respect to that matter.

CONSULTATION DURING OCP DEVELOPMENT

121) During the development of an official community plan, or the repeal or amendment of an official community plan, the proposing local government must provide one or more opportunities it considers appropriate for consultation with the persons, organizations, and authorities it considers will be affected.

ADOPTION PROCEDURES

125) An official community plan must be adopted by by-law in accordance with this section.

126) After first reading of a by-law under section 125, the local government must, in sequence, do the following:

a) consider the plan in conjunction with

i) its financial plan and

ii) any waste management plan that is applicable in the municipality or regional district;

b) hold a public hearing on the proposed official community plan.

EFFECT OF OFFICIAL COMMUNITY PLANS

127) An official community plan does not commit or authorize a municipality to proceed with any project that is specified in the plan.

128) All by-laws enacted or works undertaken by a council, after the adoption of an official community plan, must be consistent with the relevant plan.

PUBLIC HEARINGS

136) Subject to section 137, a local government must not adopt an official community plan by-law or a zoning by-law without holding a public hearing on the by-law for the purpose of allowing the public to make representations to the local government respecting matters contained in the proposed by-law.

137) The public hearing must be held after the first reading of the bylaw and before the third reading.

138) At the public hearing, all persons who believe that their interest in property is affected by the proposed by-law must be afforded a reasonable opportunity to be heard or to present written submissions respecting matters contained in the by-law that is the subject of the hearing.

139) A local government may waive the holding of a public hearing on a proposed by-law if

a) an official community plan is in effect for the area that is subject to a proposed zoning by-law and

b) the proposed by-law is consistent with the plan.

140) A council may adopt an official community plan or zoning by-law at the same meeting at which the plan or by-law passed third reading.

NOTICE OF PUBLIC HEARING

141) If a public hearing is to be held under section 136, the local government must give notice of the hearing.

PROCEDURE AFTER A PUBLIC HEARING

142) After a public hearing, the council or board may, without further notice or hearing,

a) adopt or defeat the by-law, or

b) alter and then adopt the by-law, provided that the alteration does not

i) alter the use,

ii) increase the density, or

iii) without the owner's consent, decrease the density of any area from that originally specified in the by-law.

ZONING BY-LAWS

160) A local government may, by by-law, do one or more of the following:

a) divide the whole or part of the municipality or regional district into zones, name each zone, and establish the boundaries of the zones;

b) limit the vertical extent of a zone and provide other zones above or below it;

c) regulate within a zone

i) the use of land, buildings, and other structures;

ii) the density of the use of land, buildings, and other structures;

iii) the siting, size, and dimensions of (1) buildings and other structures and (2) uses that are permitted on the land; and

iv) the location of uses on the land and within buildings and other structures;

d) regulate the shape, dimensions, and area, including the establishment of minimum and maximum sizes, of all parcels of land that may be created by subdivision, in which case

i) the regulations may be different for different areas, and

ii) the boundaries of those areas need not be the same as the boundaries of zones created under paragraph (a).

161) The authority under section 160 may be exercised by incorporating in the by-law maps, plans, tables, or other graphic material.

162) The power to regulate under section 160 includes the power to prohibit any use or uses in a zone.

PARKING SPACE REQUIREMENTS

a) A local government may, by by-law, require owners or occupiers of any land, building, or structure to provide off-street parking and loading spaces for the use, building, or structure, including spaces for use by disabled persons.

REGULATION OF SIGNS

163) Subject to the *Transportation Act* and the *Motor Vehicle Act*, a local government may, by by-law, regulate the number, size, type, form, appearance, and location of any signs.

164) A by-law under section 163 may contain different provisions for one or more of the following:

a) different zones,

b) different uses within a zone,

c) different classes of highways.

165) The power in section 163 to regulate includes the power to prohibit, except that a sign that is located on a parcel and relates to or identifies a use on that parcel must not be prohibited.

SCREENING AND LANDSCAPING TO MASK OR SEPARATE USES

166) A local government may, by by-law, require, set standards for, and regulate the provision of screening or landscaping for one or more of the following purposes:

a) masking or separating uses;

b) preserving, protecting, restoring, and enhancing the natural environment;

c) preventing hazardous conditions.

NO COMPENSATION IN RELATION TO ADOPTION OF BY-LAW OR ISSUANCE OF PERMIT

185) Compensation is not payable to any person for any reduction in the value of that person's interest in land, or for any loss or damages that result from the adoption of an official community plan or a by-law under this Division.

186) Section 185 does not apply where the by-law restricts the use of land to a public use.

ROLE PREFERENCE FORM

Instructions to students: By filling out this form, you are indicating to your instructor any special interests that you have with regard to the simulation and the extent to which you wish to participate. You are encouraged to participate to the greatest extent possible. Do not hesitate to step forward even if you feel you do not know much about local government. Every other participant in the simulation is likely to be in the same position, and this book is intended to be a guide to help you through the various stages of the simulation.

Student Name (please print): _____   _____

I would like a role that

☐ is very active,

☐ is somewhat active,

☐ is not very active.

Please indicate if there are any issues in which you are particularly interested or roles that you would like to play.

_____

_____

_____

(Note: Because several people may indicate an interest in particular roles or issues, it may not be possible for your instructor to respond to each and every expression of interest.)

Do you have any experience in local government (for example, as an elected official, employee, or actively involved citizen)? If so, please provide a brief description.

_____

_____

_____

SAMPLE BALLOT PAPER

Mark your ballot with an "**✗**."

FOR MAYOR (1 to be elected)
Name of Candidate
(last name first)

☐

Name of Candidate
(last name first)

☐

FOR COUNCIL (state number to be elected)
Name of Candidate
(last name first)

☐

Name of Candidate
(last name first)

☐

Name of Candidate
(last name first)

☐

Name of Candidate
(last name first)

☐

Name of Candidate
(last name first)

☐

CITY OF SUMMERVILLE NOMINATION PAPERS

I, _____ (insert name here), being a
citizen of Summerville; and

I, _____ (insert name here), being a
citizen of Summerville;

hereby nominate

_____(insert usual name here)

who is a citizen of Summerville

for the office of _____(state whether for mayor or councillor).

Signed at Summerville this _____ day of _____, _____

_____   _____
(signature of nominators)

I consent to this nomination.

_____
(signature of candidate)

Lightning Source UK Ltd.
Milton Keynes UK
UKHW051443160922
408974UK00019B/324